NASCAR
A CELEBRATION

First edition by Carlton Books Limited 1998

This 2002 edition published by Carlton Books Limited

20 Mortimer Street, London W1N 7RD

Text and design copyright © Carlton Books Limited 2002

Printed and bound in Italy

A CIP catalogue record for this book is available upon request.

ISBN 1 84222 453 0

Project Editor: Chris Hawkes
Project Art Editor: Zoe Maggs
Picture Research: Catherine Costelloe
Production: Sarah Corteel
Design: Graham Curd, Steve Wilson

Printed and bound in Italy

NASCAR
A CELEBRATION

BOB LATFORD

CARLTON
BOOKS

Contents

Joe Thorne
Indianapolis Motor Speedway 1938.

#6973R
Kirkpatrick
Indianapolis

His seated position belied the six foot six inch height of the man. He sat quietly amidst the swirling cigar and cigarette smoke, ignoring the din of small talk among the 35 men assembled. Deep in thought, his mind raced as he pondered the task at hand.

In the room atop the Streamline Hotel on Atlantic Avenus in Daytona Beach, Florida, he had called together an eclectic group who shared his interest in automobile racing that sunny Sunday morning in December 1947. They were bootleggers and businessmen, mechanics and merchants, some doers and some dare devils. But all shared his interest in racing, especially stock car competition.

His mind raced back to the mid-1930s when he had uprooted his wife and young son from their home in Washington D.C., left his mechanics job and headed south to Florida's warmer climate. He thought of his days as a fairly successful race car driver and his effort to both drive and promote events on the silvery sands along the Atlantic Ocean and his first race here back in 1936. With pleasure he reflected back to the July day in 1940 when he had won both the pole and the race in that big 1939 Buick. Even with the noise in the room he could hear the waves breaking on the beach a few hundred yards east of the hotel.

He thought, too, of his little gas station where he had toiled to support his family and his racing; of the gas rationing during the war which had concluded two years earlier and had cut so badly into the station's business; of his work during those war years at the local boat works where he had utilized his mechanical skills to build submarine chasers as part of the war effort. Smiling a little, he recalled how racing had resumed not long after the hostilities ended and the final foe had signed a surrender.

In post-war America the families were reunited. Returning veterans had money in their pockets and the industry of war was reverting to making peacetime goods. Racing, with the end of gas rationing and other shortages, had resumed the year before. New groups had been formed to sanction and promote events. Each of them was making its own rules and proclaiming their best as the "National Stock Car Champion". The public and news media were confused as to who was the real champion.

Nodding to the assembled group the tall man, still sitting, began to speak. His deep, strong voice hushed the remaining conversations.

Even in 1947, when William Henry Getty "Big Bill" France spoke, people listened.

"Nothing stands still in this world. Things get better or worse, bigger or smaller.

"Stock car racing has been my whole life. I've gone to other territories; I've left home, and I've always tried to develop something as I was going. I've tried to build up instead of tearing down."

He went on to explain his background and his philosophy on the sport he loved. Then continued as he explained why he had asked them to be at this meeting.

"There are a whole lot of things to be straightened out here. We've got to get track owners and promoters interested in building up stock car racing. I would like to get all of us in accord on as many different subjects as we can bring up.

"Stock car racing as we've been running it is not, in my opinion, the answer. If it were, I wouldn't worry about anybody else...

"I believe stock car racing can become a nationally-recognized sport by having a national point standing which will embrace the majority of large stock car events. Regardless of whether you win a race in New England or Florida, the points would apply in the national championship bracket. What it would amount to is we'd have a national champion who won his spurs on a national championship basis."

France touched on a few other points, and concluded his brief, but tone-setting remarks, by saying, "This touches about everything I had in mind. Right here, within our group, rests the outcome of stock car racing in the country today. We have the opportunity to set it up on a big scale. We are interested in one thing—improving present conditions."

The room erupted in a hub-bub of reaction, accompanied with nods of agreement with what had been said.

With enthusiasm they went to work. Over the rest of that day and the next two, they hammered out rules, by-laws and guidelines for their sport. Jerome "Red" Vogt, already a noted and successful mechanic came up with a suggestion for the name of the organization: National Association for Stock Car Auto Racing. It was a title which reflected the scope (National), type (Stock Car), and purpose (Racing) of the new group. It would replace the National Champion Stock Car Circuit moniker France had used for his events previously and whose initials—NCSCC—did not spell anything. Someone else suggested National Stock Car Racing Association (NSCRA), but it was found that another competing group had already used that name. Vogt's suggestion was accepted. NASCAR it would be.

Among the final items of business were electing officers and getting the group incorporated. France, who had introduced himself as the meeting's "director" was immediately voted in as the president. Eddie Blank of Jacksonville, Fla., was vice-president, Bill Tuthill, a former motorcycle racer and promoter was named secretary and the local driver Marshall Teague was voted in as the first treasurer. The group suggested the creation of a "Czar" for the sport. E.G. "Cannonball" Baker, who had become famous for a cross-country speed run and other racing successes, was a good choice. France called him at his Indianapolis home and he accepted, but the title was changed to "Commissioner" due to conflicts with Russian policies of the era. Finally, France asked local Daytona Beach attorney, Louis Ossinsky (who had his office across Main Street from France's Amoco gas station) to draw up the legal paperwork to finalize the newly- constructed group. [Your author and his brothers, on our way home from school, parked our bicycles outside the hotel and were in the room when France called Baker.]

They had determined there would be three divisions to start the 1948 inaugural season under the NASCAR banner. They would continue to race the pre-war coupes and sedans with engine "tinkering" allowed in the Modified division. Also they would continue to have events for the low-slung Roadsters and they would have a new headlining "Strictly Stock" division for the post-war cars. The latter would not only be the name for the series of events, but also define the amount of alterations which would be permitted on the cars.

> **Having agreed on the name NASCAR, the newly-formed organization starts to take shape**

Further consideration delayed the new car division's birth. So soon after the war, new cars were still in short supply as the auto manufacturers struggled to get supply up to demand as they continued to shift factories from the production of tanks, jeeps and other combat needs over to making street cars for the public. France and his cohorts reasoned the public would not want to watch, as the cars they could not yet obtain, were beat up and dinged on race tracks. For 1948's campaign, at least, the older Modified cars would serve as the featured division for the foundling sanctioning body.

The first race was scheduled on a new beach-and-road course further south of the layout utilized from the mid-1930s through 1947, the one where France himself had raced and won. Post-war development of the area precluded its continued use as homes and motels sprang up in a construction boom. The new location was not yet being developed. A course which used a two-mile stretch of sandy beach, packed by the high ocean tides, to connect to an equal distance of paved two-lane highway A1A was constructed. Crushed limestone was brought in and packed to create turns at either end.

More than 60 entries from a dozen states were received at the new organization's headquarters. Some 50 of them showed up and were on the beach to get the starting signal on February 15, 1948. Fearing a massive first-lap pile-up by the massive field, France elected to send them off in waves at one second intervals. Teague, the elected treasurer of NASCAR and a home-town hero, as well as a World War II Air Force Flight Engineer and now a local Pure Oil gas station operator, jumped his 1939 Ford out from its front-row starting position and became the first driver to lead a lap in NASCAR history. Fonty Flock, also piloting a '39 Ford, outdid his brothers Tim and Bob in the race, as he created the first NASCAR lead change by getting around Teague in the 35th of the 68 laps. Teague retook the lead when Flock flipped while enjoying nearly a half-mile advantage. Teague encountered fading breaks on his mount as the laps waned. Robert "Red" Byron, behind the wheel of the '39 Ford, as were most of the starters that day, dogged Teague's tire tracks as they fought their way through the rutted turns and around slower cars. As they approached the car of Mickey Rhodes, who was having trouble bumping his way through the soft sand in the North Turn, they split the slower car. Teague drove to the inside and Byron went high to maintain his momentum.

Byron, a shrapnel-wounded tail gunner during the war who had to have his left foot fixed to a stirrup attached to the clutch pedal, made the right choice as he assumed the lead and was never headed as he took a 15-second victory over Teague to become the first winner of a NASCAR-sanctioned race. (Although run under the organization's sanction, the actual incorporation of NSACAR was not finalized until Febraury 21, a half dozen days after the race was conducted.)

That was the first of 52 NASCAR races held that season at 20 tracks from Florida to Pennsylvania. They were won by 14 different drivers, including all three siblings from the Flock family. While Fonty Flock's 15 victories headed the season's winner's list, Byron collected ten more checkered flags to go with the one earned at Daytona. Between them they won the final seven races of that inaugural season (Byron won four, Flock won three) as Byron emerged as the first champion. His season's triumph earned his car owner, Raymond Parks of Atlanta, the first championship owner in the organization's history and Vogt, Byron's primary wrench twister, the initial championship mechanic for the organization he had named.

New Cars

The success of the 1948 season caused France's sun-tanned face to crinkle as he smiled. The competition had been good. The rules were adhered to and the public liked what they had seen.

Now, in the second year, the novelty of the sport had waned. They had to maintain the standards created in 1948 and they had to grow. He noticed more cars were appearing in the parking lots at the tracks. He had had to notice as he was often out in the lots helping unprepared promoters get the crowds in. He sold tickets, stubbed them, parked cars, addressed driver's meetings, oversaw rules disputes and anything else he needed to do to make his sport successful. But the growth of the new model cars bringing fans to the tracks really registered in his agile mind.

Maybe it was time to try out the "Strictly Stock" concept he presented at the 1947 meeting. As the 1949 season began, he worked on the concept. New cars, showroom stock. No, they won't take the beating these dirt tracks give. OK, we'll let them bolster the right front wheel, the one that takes the brunt of the stress in the turns. Let them put a steel plate in it to keep the lug nuts from ripping through the wheel. But that's all! The rest has to be just as it came from a dealer's showroom floor. They'll have to tape over the head lights and tail lights. Broken glass could cut tires. We'll have to make them strap the doors shut so that drivers don't get thrown out and tie down the hoods and trunks so they don't go flapping open on the rougher tracks.

Early in the 1949 season, some drivers entered newer cars, post-war models in the Modified races, but with little success. France tried an exhibition event for his "Strictly Stock" class as part of a triple header at Broward Speedway, a two-mile oval just north of Miami. It was a five-lap, ten-mile race as part of the undercard for a 100-mile Grand Prix Roadster race in late February. Area driver Benny Georgeson, in a new Buick, won it over Ohio's Eddie Mitchell who drove a Mercury. It was not an impressive race. Most forgot it in the shadow of the bigger event.

At the same time, early 1949, France's organization was being challenged for drivers and cars by the National Stock Car Racing Association (NSCRA) of O. Bruton Smith, who now heads Speedway Motorsports which owns

Charlotte, Atlanta, Bristol and other interests. France quickly resumed his push for the Strictly Stock division, scheduling a race for the three-quarter mile dirt oval in Charlotte, North Carolina where his Modifieds had raced in 1948. It would be a long-distance race—300 laps, run June 19, and have a whopping $5,000 in posted awards at stake. A field of cars woud not be hard to get, he reasoned, since the concept allowed hopefuls to drive their entry right from the dealership to the track. He assured himself a full line-up of 33 cars would be on hand. He was right. They were.

On Saturday, June 19, he had them run time trials to arrange the field of starters. Bob Flock, in a 1946 Hudson, was the quickest of the day. The eldest of the three Atlanta brothers circled the track at 67.958 mph to outrun his youngest sibling, Tim, in a new Oldsmobile and Red Byron, now in a new Olds owned by Raymond Parks and tuned by Red Vogt. Coverall-clad Otis Martin put his 1948 Ford fourth in the line-up with Fonty Flock, the middle brother, to round out the top five in a '49 Hudson.

Starting 12th in the race was a young Lincoln-driving Kansan, named Jim Roper. He drove the car from his home state after learning of the race from a plug placed in the *Smiling Jack* comic strip by artist Zack Mosely. Mosely was a fellow Floridian and friend of France who often plugged the races as well as air shows in his drawings. The panel of the strip Roper saw merely said "Stock Car Race, June 19, Charlotte, N.C.", but it was enough to catch Roper's eye and head him east.

Also in the line-up, in 13th place behind Roper, was Georgia's Sara Christian who drove her husband's '47 Ford along with the male drivers in their Buicks, Chryslers, Hudsons, Mercurys, Olsmobiles, Fords and a Kaiser. Black was the predominant car color, but there were also a few gray, red, a green one and some with no paint at all. Every car carried an identifying number on its sides, hand painted or applied with masking tape.

As the noon opening gates approached, long lines of traffic had already assembled. The jam was so great, France opened the gates early to let them in. Some estimates of attendance were as high as 22,000-plus. It was a grand beginning and proof that France's concept was being well received.

Raceday dawned clear and bright over the scruffy wooden fences that surrounded the red dirt oval. The 33 cars coughed and snarled as they took the pre-race pace and parade laps. The crowd was standing as the pace car dropped to the side and the green flag flew to start the race.

The eldest Flock proved his pole-winning effort was indicative of his race prowess. He jumped into the lead at the start and his hulking Hudson kicked up a rooster tail of red dust for the followers to battle, along with each other. Flock was ahead for the first five trips around the three-quarter-mile oval when, through the dust, came the black hood and white side-walled tires of a Lincoln driven by Bill Blair. Soon thereafter Flock headed for the pits, his engine dripping oil and done for the day. Mechanical failures were commonplace, as was overheating, when dirt-clogged radiators quickly geysered steam and ended the hopes of many drivers.

The only mishap of the race came in the 107th lap. Lee Petty, who'd driven the family's Buick to the race, flipped over in the third turn. The car ended up on all four tires, but the dismayed Petty walked away wondering how he would explain the damage to his wife back home in Randleman, N.C., and how he would get his young sons Richard and Maurice back to the family farm.

While others fell by the wayside, Blair pressed his advantage. Cruising over the rough track and bouncing through the rapidly developing pot holes, he soon lapped all the other surviving cars. But the attrition rate took him in, too, just 50 laps shy of the 200 circuit's needed to collect the $2,000 first-place plum. A dejected Blair nursed the steam-spewing Lincoln to a stop in the pits and was denied a place in the sport's history.

One man's luck is another's misfortune and vice-versa. Blair's departure opened the door, seemingly, for Glenn Dunnaway from nearby Gastonia, N.C. He had arrived at the track race morning and was tapped by Hubert Westmoreland to drive his Ford, since Dunnaway was more familiar with the track.

The black Ford made up the lap deficit quickly and was ahead of the field for the final 50 laps. At the checkered flag, Dunnaway was three full laps ahead of Roper's Lincoln.

But the drama wasn't over. In post-race inspections, overseen by NASCAR officials to make certain the cars were strictly stock, the rear springs on the Dunnaway–Westmoreland Ford were found to have been "spread" or stiffened. It was an old trick employed by bootleggers so revenue agents would not see the back of the cars sagging under the loads of moonshine in the trunk.

The Ford was disqualified. Roper, by virtue of his attention to detail in his comic-strip reading, was elevated to first place and became the first winner in the history of the new NASCAR division. Fonty Flock, who had been flagged home in third was elevated to second and Byron upped to third. Mrs Christian, with relief help from Bob Flock, was listed in 14th place on the final finishing order.

The race had been a huge success. France's dream had come to reality. More were quickly scheduled. In early July they ran a 166-mile battle on the beach-and-road course in Daytona with Byron winning over a field that included three females. Christian was joined by Louise Smith who drove her husband's Ford and Ethel Flock Mobley, also driving a Cadillac owned by her husband, Charles. Ethel's presence made the race unique as the field had four of the Flock children competing. Tim Flock finished second to Byron to have the best performance by a member of the family quartet, but Ethel finished ahead of her brothers Bob and Fonty—a fact she never let them forget.

More races were scheduled by France, taking full advantage of the surge of popularity. In August at Hillsborough, N.C., with Bob Flock winning. Early September had them racing on the circular mile at Langhorne, P.A., where Curtis Turner triumphed. A week later the new cars battled in the half-mile oval at Hamburg, N.Y., with Jack White the winner and a week later the site was Martinsville, V.A., with Byron winning again. As October began, Pittsburgh's Heidelburg Speedway saw Lee Petty giving Plymouth a first win and the eighth and final event of that inaugural season came at North Wilkesboro, N.C., with the victory earned by Bob Flock.

Through the events of the year, Byron's hard driving and consistency allowed him and his Raymond Parks-owned team to amass the greatest number of points and earn the champion's crown—plus a $1,000 check that went with it. The group, with Red Vogt still utilizing his mechanical skills on the car, thus became the first champions.

Growth in the 1950s

With the tentative start of its new car division a success, NASCAR moved into the 1950s strongly. The popular competition for the newest and best of Detroit's production lines had a new name, "Grand National". It was borrowed from European horse racing and was intended to signify superior qualities.

"The 'Strictly Stock' name was more a guideline for the rules," France explained. "Grand National is a more dynamic label that has more appeal to the public."

The division's popularity and acceptance had tracks clamoring for a place on the schedule. The eight 1949 races quickly grew to more than double that number. There were 19 in 1950 and 41 by 1951. Included in the 1950 slate of events was a new one at a brand new mile-and-a-quarter track in Darlington, South Carolina. It would be a 500- mile event, the longest ever attempted by the cars or drivers, and the track was paved in an era when all prior races had been contested on dirt surfaces. They spent two weeks qualifying the 75-car field, with officials feeling they needed that number to make certain some were still running at the end. It was a rousing success with Johnny Mantz, the slowest qualifier, bringing a Plymouth home to victory as the first 500-mile winner in stock car history.

The 1951 campaign saw the circuit expand beyond its predominantly Southeastern area. Races were added in Arizona, on the west coast in California and in the midwest in Ohio and Michigan.

The 1951 campaign opened in Daytona with hometown driver Marshall Teague winning the 160-mile event on the beach and road course in his Hudson Hornet. In post race inspection the NASCAR officials found they did not have a copy of the car's factory specifications. They called the Hudson company to get them. It was only then the firm's executives learned one of their cars had won a big stock car race. After sending the engineering sheets to the NASCAR officials, the company invited the winning driver to Michigan. Teague, an erudite former Air Force flight engineer, so impressed the Hudson officials they agreed to provide him with cars and parts to continue his racing. The resultant publicity was read by Pure Oil Company executives in Chicago where they learned the big Daytona winner was also the owner-operator of one of their gas stations in Daytona. They, too, invited Teague and his wife Mitzi to the corporate offices. There Teague also convinced Pure Oil to supply gas and lubricants for the races. Thus was created the first factory support from a manufacturer and the first contingency program by a supplier in the sport's history.

Another of the pivotal events was held that August on the state fairgrounds in Detroit. The 250-mile contest drew a large field of 59 cars representing some 15 makes of car. It also attracted a large contingent of automobile executives from the various corporate offices for the event which celebrated the 250th anniversary of Detroit's founding. The race became a slugfest as the cars beat and banged over the rough dirt surface. It also became a period of chagrin for the coat-and-tie bunch representing the auto makers as they watched their machines fail mechanically and become involved in numerous wrecks due to suspension malfunctions. The manufacturers' brass vowed to cease the

Rough and tumble: Flips and wrecks were common in the early days as seen here on the North turn of the Beach-Road course in Daytona

embarrassment by supplying stronger parts and more reliable engines. It was the birth of performance parts.

As the NASCAR division continued to grow and expand the winning drivers emerged as sports stars. Names like Teague, Lee Petty, the Flock brothers and Curtis Turner were emerging as heroes to the ever-growing number of fans.

By the middle of the decade a new face came on the stock car scene in the person of wealthy midwesterner Carl Kiekhaefer. The owner of Mercury Outboard marine engines felt his company's name emblazoned on winning cars would enhance sales. He came with not just one car but a stable of white Chrysler 300s and enlisted the top drivers to

pilot them. He also had the cars trucked from race to race and they were attended by a staff of uniformed mechanics.

Chevrolet and Ford also jumped into the sport with big-buck programs. Both felt on-track success would result in additional sales for their brand at dealerships. It did. By the end of the 1955 season Mauri Rose headed the Chevrolet operation and 1925 Indianapolis 500 winner Pete DePaolo was the leader of Ford's racing program. Mercury joined in with Californian Bill Stroppe in charge of their effort, and Lee Petty had the Plymouth endeavor.

But it was the big white Chryslers which dominated as Kiekhaefer's cars won 22 of the 40 races they entered, with Tim Flock taking 18 of them and adding 18 poles in taking the series title.

In the midst of the unparalleled success of NASCAR tragedy struck. In the 1955 Le Mans 24-hour race in France, a car went off course and into the crowd. Nearly 100 spectators were killed. Politicians called for the ban of all forms of auto racing. But NASCAR's strength, Bill France's determination and the support of the car makers allowed stock car racing to continue. It not only extended its run, the growth swelled as well.

The factories continued their "Win on Sunday, sell on Monday" approach until another tragedy hit stock car racing when a car went off the track at Martinsville and killed an eight year old boy who was in an area plainly marked "No Spectators Allowed". The resultant publicity drove the factories, already under media pressure for promoting horsepower, away. The manufacturers gave the racing equipment to the drivers. Kiekhaefer had left the circuit after the 1956 season when he felt resentment of this domination was hurting the sales of his boat motors.

But the sport continued to grow to a fifty-three race 1957 schedule at tracks from coast to coast. New faces were frequenting victory lanes. Buck Baker, Speedy Thompson, Bob Welborn, Fireball Roberts and Junior Johnson emerged as hard charging winners.

During the decade the sanctioning body also tried new divisions. A Short Track segment was introduced in 1951 to give tracks of less than half a mile a place on the docket, and in 1955 NASCAR acquired the midwest SAFE (Society of Autosports Fellowship and Education) group for its convertible circuit. They also tried their hand at Speedway cars with a division for the open-wheeled cars that ran at Indianapolis equipped with stock car engines. They also dabbled in Midgets, drag racing and sports car events and started a Sportsman division which was similar in appearance to the Modifieds but allowed less experimentation and were not as expensive. Most were short lived—the Speedway cars lasted just two seasons, the Convertibles three before being absorbed in the Grand National fold. The Sportsman survived to later become the Late Model Sportsman and finally the current Busch Grand National Series.

A big change in the sport's future started at the end of the decade with the 1959 opening of the 2.5-mile tri-oval Daytona International Speedway in Florida. It was the biggest and fastest facility the NASCAR drivers had ever seen or contended with. It proved to be a huge success, too, as the first Daytona 500 came down to a photo finish between Johnny Beauchamp and Lee Petty. It took three days of studying photos of them crossing the finish line to determine Petty the winner by inches. It was the closest finish in any 500-mile race to that point in motorsports history.

Stock car racing had not just survived its formative years, it had mushroomed far beyond its founder's dreams. And it wasn't through.

Ready for a three-abreast start at the 1953 racing in Dover Motor Speedway.

New places, new faces in the 1960s

The opening of the Daytona track at the end of the 1950s led to a surge of new tracks being built specifically to hold NASCAR events. The 1960 season saw the mile-and-a-half tracks come on line at Charlotte, North Carolina and in Atlanta, Georgia. The following year marked the start of the half-mile oval in Bristol, Tennessee. It was a growth spurt that lasted throughout the decade. In 1965 the new mile "D" shaped North Carolina Motor Speedway opened its gates at Rockingham and 1969 saw four more tracks come on the NASCAR line including the mile oval in Dover, Delaware, a two-mile track in Brooklyn, Michigan, the 2.66-mile, 33-degree banked super speedway at Talladega, Alabama and a two-mile track at College Station, Texas.

It was a time, too, which found the factory backing returned covertly and new stars emerging in the racing skies. Many of the pioneer drivers had retired but replacing them came young stars like Richard Petty, Cale Yarborough, David Pearson and the Allison brothers, Bobby and Donnie.

But the landscape of the sport encountered bumps, too. This was the span which saw drivers like Joe Weatherly and Fireball Roberts become fatality statistics due to racing accidents. It was also the time when the car makers tried to make the rules conform to their desires.

In 1964 the Chrysler cars showed up with the potent engines with hemispherical combustion chambers. Richard Petty used one to win the Daytona 500 and go on to win his first championship. When NASCAR took steps to reduce the exotic "hemi" after the season, Chrysler withdrew its cars from NASCAR competition in 1965. The following year Ford tried to use a limited-edition dual overhead cam power plant for the races, only to have it banned. Ford pulled out of the 1965 campaign. But NASCAR persevered through the effort of promoters like Charlotte's Richard Howard. The portly track president and general manager produced a covey of Chevrolets to replace the Chrysler products in 1965 and the following year lured top Ford drivers—Curtis Turner, Ned Jarrett and Marvin Panch—away to drive other cars. Panch went on to win the May 600-miler at Charlotte in a second Petty Plymouth.

Among the first of the new stars to emerge was David Pearson. The 1960 Rookie of the Year entered the 1961 season without a ride. He was quickly tapped by master mechanic Ray Fox to fill the seat in his factory supported Pontiac. Pearson promptly scored his breakthrough triumph in the World 600 at Charlotte and went on to win two more super speedway races at Daytona and Atlanta for the first three wins of a 105-victory career. Pearson's trio of victories had the media calling him "Little David the Giant Killer" for winning three big races in a season, an unprecedented feat in 1961. Pearson would win his first championship in 1966 while driving Dodges for Cotton Owens and two more at the end of the decade behind the wheel of a Holman-Moody factory Ford. The second generation of the Petty clan, Richard, would also claim the first of his seven titles during the decade and Ned Jarrett won both of his during the span before retiring at the end of the 1966 season.

It was a decade which saw many safety innovations made to the sport. Shoulder harnesses mandatorily supplemented the lap belt for driver safety. Driver compartment roll cages were augmented to strengthen the protective steel cocoon surrounding the driver's seat. Fuel cells were added to gas tanks to reduce the threat of fire, such as had claimed Fireball Roberts. Tire inner-liners were added to reduce wrecks caused by blow-outs and fire-retardant driving suits replaced the cotton shirt and duck pants worn by most of the speed merchants.

The schedule of events continued to swell and reached a zenith during the 1964 campaign when 62 races were held. Part of the slate was a heat-escaping swing to northern tracks in New Jersey, New York and Pennsylvania following the July 4th race at Daytona. It was on the 1964 "Northern Tour" that Texan Billy Wade won four straight races, a first in the division's history and one topped by Richard Petty three years later when he won ten consecutive events to set a mark which still stands. Petty won his second title in that 1967 season when he won 27 races, also a record which is unlikely to be broken.

Other drivers were also emerging. Ford's "Fearless Freddy" Lorenzen was challenging Plymouth's Petty in the mid-1960s and toward the end of the decade Cale Yarborough began putting the Wood brothers' Ford in victory lanes with regularity. In the decade's latter years another "Yarb" emerged as LeeRoy Yarbrough took the seat in Junior Johnson's Ford to count Daytona, Charlotte, Darlington and Atlanta among his seven 1969 triumphs.

The sport attracted more media attention as the decade moved along. July's Daytona race in 1961, then called

the Firecracker 250 and now the Pepsi 400, was televised by ABC's *Wide World of Sports* and more national media attention was afforded the now-established sport of stock car racing under the NASCAR banner.

The racing surfaces were changing, too. At its start the sport ran mostly on dirt tracks. As the new big tracks entered the picture they came with asphalt surfaces. Most of the early drivers had come from dirt track racing where they man-handled the cars, and where power-sliding through the turns was the way to race. The paved tracks required different talents. Some of the pioneers could not adjust and fell by the wayside. Others could and joined the fresh new faces for the ride on the crest of the wave of new-found popularity in the sport. The decade marked great change. In 1959 just 17 of the 44 races were contested on paved tracks. Ten years later saw just five of the 54 races in the 1969 season held on tracks with a dirt surface. None of the winners from the 1959 season were still regulars in the sport a decade later.

Bill France's sport was growing up. It had developed muscles and new wrinkles. Smooth competition was replacing the rough and tumble of infancy. The child had found a measure of maturity with its new playgrounds and safer toys.

To many veterans it was sad to lose the exuberance of youth and to say goodbye to the collection of colorful characters who had helped the sport grow. But the wiser observers understood how some of that changing would help open the doors to a wider national acceptance. But even they couldn't foresee what the future would bring to the rapidly flourishing sport of NASCAR stock car racing.

The 1970s

While NASCAR had seen a lot of changes in the 1950s and '60s, they were nowhere near the magnitude that awaited in the next decade. Changes in leadership, quantity of events, media coverage and support sources for the racing teams all converged on the sport during the 1970s.

It seemed the ten years were off to a bad beginning when the Ford and Chrysler factories withdrew in the opening years. They had been the suppliers of parts, engineering and funds for the top teams. Those teams would, in turn, hand down parts and pieces to the smaller teams. Without the factory backing it was feared the supply chain would be greatly impacted. Other help would be needed.

However, as the factories went away another major firm, tobacco giant R. J. Reynolds, entered the scene and a pact was formed with ABC-TV to show some of the races, albeit taped, nationally.

The entry of Reynolds, through their Winston brand, took a circuitous route. Junior Johnson, the noted former driver and top car owner, had approached them as a potential sponsor. After listening to the firm's marketing plans and future goals, Johnson directed them to the NASCAR headquarters in Daytona Beach for a meeting with Bill France, Sr. The sanctioning body and cigarette maker reached an agreement and NASCAR's Grand National Division was on its way to becoming the Winston Cup Series.

Other teams, and Johnson's, too, were able to convince additional businesses to join them as sponsors. The convincing of consumer goods makers to put their names on cars and provide the needed funding to operate a top-line race team was aided by the television package which had been forged on NASCAR's behalf by Richard Howard of Charlotte Motor Speedway.

A bombshell fell on the sport early in 1972 when Bill France, Sr, the founder and only president NASCAR had known since its 1948 inception, announced in early February he was stepping down and turning the reins over to his oldest son, William Clifton France, more familiarly known as Bill Jr. The older France was 62 at the time. His son was 38 and had spent his whole adult life in and around the sport.

The 1972 campaign would be a different one. The Winston folks had lent their support to just the 1971 events of 250 miles or longer. It was announced at the end of 1971 that the Winston Cup Grand National Division would consist of only those longer, more important races in the 1972 season and thereafter. Where there had been 44 races in 1971 there would be just 31 that season with each one supported by billboards and special newspaper advertising placed by the tobacco firm. Winston would also post a whopping $100,000 point fund. The change meant many of the short tracks which had presented the 100–125 mile events would no longer be part of the program. Instead, NASCAR created a Grand National East Division to supplant the loss.

The 1970s was a decade of great change in the NASCAR world

The decade's transitions involved drivers, too. Many of the sports super stars of the '60s were retired. New faces took their place. One was a brash youngster from Tennessee named Darrell Waltrip. Another came with his red hair from the red hills of northern Georgia named Bill Elliott. Ricky Rudd entered the scene from Virginia. An indication of the change was found in the 1970 Daytona 500 when a blond former Modified Division star from Dedham,

Massachusetts named Pete Hamilton drove a winged Petty Plymouth to victory in the big event. Some of the sport's stars who established themselves in the prior decade continued to win most of the races. Richard Petty was still there, as was Buddy Baker. David Pearson was also continuing his winning ways, but the new faces were showing up in the top-five places at the end of the races. Waltrip started winning as did Neil Bonnett and Benny Parsons.

The rules were being tinkered with as the sport's technology advanced. The first carburetor restrictor plates were introduced in 1970 to slow the cars at all venues. Engine sizes were cut back from the 430 cubic inch upper limit and wider, untreaded tires became the sport's norm during the time span. Racing became a good citizen as one of the few sports to curtail energy consumption during the fuel crisis in the decade's early years. NASCAR opted to reduce early 1974 races by ten percent even though studies showed racing used less fuel than most other sports which were conducted in lighted and heated/air conditioned facilities.

In the middle of the decade NASCAR found its point systems too complicated for either fans or competitors to understand. They had tried four methods in nine years and frequently employed methods whereby money, track size or race length made no two events carry the same value toward the season's championship.

In August 1974, at the Talladega race, they asked your author to come up with a new system. After gathering records, data and information from Joe Whitlock and Phil Holmer at the NASCAR offices in Florida, the current system was devised and tested against prior years' events. It was simple. Every race had the same weight in determining the standings regardless of track length, race distance, or posted awards. First place in every race would be worth 175 points and drop by five between each of the top five places, by four between the next five and by three through last place. Additionally each leader of a race would get five bonus points and the leader of the most laps got another five. (The latter was for great early drivers like Curtis Turner, Junior Johnson and Fireball Roberts who always ran for the lead and drew huge numbers of fans but were not rewarded for their efforts under any of the prior point systems.) The system was adopted and has been in effect from the start of the 1975 campaign throughout the balance of the sport's first 50 seasons.

The decade also saw some new tracks arrive. The three-turn 2.5-mile Pocono International Raceway in Pennsylvania became part of the circuit in 1974 and earlier another rectangular 2.5-mile track at Ontario, California started presenting NASCAR races. The last dirt track race was held at the decade's start. It was in 1970 on a half-mile oval at Raleigh, North Carolina with Richard Petty the winner. By the end of the decade the move toward bigger tracks became clear. By the 1978 season all but six of the facilities that held Winston Cup events were a mile or longer in length.

The '70s saw an unprecedented feat and one unmatched as the sport's major league completed its 50th season.

In 1976, 1977 and 1979 the only champion was Cale Yarborough who won all three titles driving the cars fielded by Junior Johnson.

The end of the decade produced a pivotal moment for the sport. Late in 1978 Bill France, Jr, and CBS-TV executives announced the 1979 Daytona 500 would be shown live, flag-to-flag by the network. It was an unprecedented commitment by a major network. It was also a move benefited by a snowstorm which locked in much of the eastern half of the country. The race unfolded under dreary Florida skies as the snowbound television viewers watched. The race came down to a shoot-out between Yarborough and Donnie Allison. The two had spun-out early in the race but made up lost laps to take the white flag in a side-by-side battle for the lead. They spun again as they exited the second turn for the final time in a wreck that lasted all the way down the long back straightaway and into the third turn where the two cars, now wrecked, stopped. As Richard Petty and Darrell Waltrip swept by, Yarborough and Allison got out of their cars and began to fight. Petty went on to score his sixth victory in the prestigious event as he nosed out a hard

charging Waltrip. Bobby Allison stopped at the wreck to check on his younger brother only to also become involved in the fisticuffs, all caught by the television cameras. The great racing and powerful human drama sent the telecast's rating through the roof, handily beating opposing shows.

It started a trend which has seen all Winston Cup races getting full live coverage on network and cable television and still drawing top ratings among sports events, even though the audiences are no longer snowbound.

The 1970s saw NASCAR continue not only to grow but also bloom into a sport of national significance under Bill France Junior's new guidance. The schedule of fewer events had made each one more important. The new sponsorships extended the sport's impact beyond the grandstands and into the market place. The television coverage had placed it into the nation's homes.

As the decade closed it did so on a bigger, better brand of stock car racing under the NASCAR banner.

The 1980s

As a new decade dawned NASCAR had emerged as the largest, most competitive and lucrative form of racing on earth. The tracks and starting fields were full, the names of corporate America were broadly shown from the sides of race cars and viewers at home were watching the races unfold on their television sets.

But the tracks' attendance figures showed little growth. It was hard to do when all the seats were full. They would add seating each season but a few thousand seats in a 60,000-seat facility doesn't bring the growth rate up much. Grand expansion was needed and it came toward the end of the decade.

It was a period when the boisterous antics of the colorful early drivers would be replaced by the glib

> **The largest, most competitive and most lucrative form of racing on earth**

correctness of the corporate image. Drivers had to speak well as well as drive. The athletes of racing had to be able to address a national sales meeting as smoothly as they might discuss springs and shock absorbers or gear ratios with their crew chief. Even event names were having commercial identification added to them.

**Suppliers saw the value of NASCAR to develop,
test and market their products**

Charlotte's World 600 became the Coca Cola 600, Atlanta's Dixie 500 was changed to the Atlanta Journal-Constitution 500 and the venerable Southern 500 at Darlington became the Heinz 500.

More new faces emerged. The first was a 27 year old from Kannapolis, North Carolina who scored his first big track win in Atlanta in 1980. It was Dale Earnhardt in only his sophomore season. He was just in front of another newcomer that day when Rusty Wallace finished second in his first Winston Cup start. Earnhardt would go on to take the Cup crown, the first of the seven he'd win over the next decade and a half. Darrell Waltrip had left DiGard Racing and had moved into the seat vacated at the end of 1980 by Cale Yarborough. Waltrip drove the Junior Johnson machines to the driving championships during his first two years as Johnson's chauffeur. Terry Labonte had come on the scene in the late 1970s and broke into the sport's winning column with a victory in the 1980 Labor Day classic at Darlington.

The old guard was still there, too. Yarborough continued to win in his new ride with the M.C. Anderson team and so did Richard Petty. Big Buddy Baker, now behind the wheel of Harry Ranier's car, won the fastest Daytona 500 in history when he led the way to the 1980 event's checkered flag with a winning average of 177.602mph. It was the fastest stock car event ever run at the time and a record which still stood as the fastest Daytona 500 ever as NASCAR concluded its 50th season nearly two decades later.

The rewards were growing apace with the sport's increasing popularity. The Winston Cup point fund had begun at $100,000 when introduced in 1971. By the start of the 1980s it was a quarter million dollars and swelled to $2.5 million by the decade's end.

In the middle of the decade Winston announced a new lucrative program. They offered, starting in 1985, a $1 million bonus that would be paid to any driver winning three of the sport's "Big Four" races: The Daytona 500, the biggest, The Winston 500, The Coca Cola 600, the longest, and Darlington's Southern 500, the oldest. The timing couldn't have been better for Bill Elliott, a lanky Ford driver from Dawsonville, Georgia. At the time of the program's introduction at the annual post-season awards ceremony, which was by this time held in the Grand Ball Room of New

York's Waldorf-Astoria Hotel, Elliott had won just four times over his nine years in the major league. In 1985 he went on a tear. His 11 1985 wins included three of the four involved in the bonus (he did not win the 600) and Elliott became "Million Dollar Bill".

Elliott's dramatic success didn't earn him the season's crown. In fact his season waned after the big payday. The crown went to Waltrip who parlayed three wins and a very consistent season-long performance to garner his third championship.

In the course of the campaign Winston also slated a "winner's-only" invitational race at Charlotte in May, the day prior to the 600-mile classic. "The Winston" would boast a field of Winston Cup race winners from the 1984 campaign and up through the Talladega race run earlier that month, and would pay the winner a cool $200,000. Waltrip was the inaugural winner and went on to take the next day's 600 as well. Both times he had to run down and pass a determined Harry Gant for the victories.

Both Waltrip and Elliott picked up bonus checks at the 1985 banquet in New York to raise their season's winnings above the $1 million mark. It was the first time a driver had won a million or more in a season. NASCAR racing had come a long way.

As the money went up so did the speeds, especially at the big Daytona and Talladega tracks. In 1982 Benny Parsons had become the first NASCAR driver to qualify above the 200-mile-an-hour mark as he won the pole at Talladega with a run of 200.176 for the spring race. Two years later Cale Yarborough time trialed above that plateau at Daytona. By 1987 Elliott had jumped the overall record to 212.809 in May at Talladega. But the race saw Bobby Allison's engine let go in the track's tri-oval. Pieces from the

detonated power plant cut his car's rear tires and it spun, launching into the protective mesh grandstand fence at the flagman's stand, tearing down a large section and coming precariously close to going into the spectator area before settling back on the track.

The near disaster so alarmed NASCAR officials they immediately imposed carburetor restrictor plates on the cars to reduce the air-gas mix to the engines and slow the cars for future races at both the Talladega and Daytona tracks. The plates have been in use and adjusted to keep the speeds below the 200mph level ever since.

Other new winners emerged in the 1980s. In 1983 Ricky Rudd won twice. Those victories began a string of winning seasons which was still intact 16 years later. A colorful and dashing driver from Ohio came to the NASCAR ranks after winning Rookie honors in the Indy 500 as Tim Richmond added his name to the sanctioning body's winners' list in the middle of the decade. A second and a third generation driver also emerged on the scene during the decade as Bobby Allison's son Davey joined his father and uncle with victories in the sport's major league, and Kyle Petty joined his father and grandfather, Richard and Lee, respectively, as a winner in Winston Cup competition.

There were new faces behind the pit wall at the tracks during the decade, too. New owners emerged. Some were former drivers, but many were men with acumen in other businesses. People like car dealer Rick Hendrick, who started in 1984 with veteran crew-chief Harry Hyde and driver Geoff Bodine and by 1986 they had won the Daytona 500. Cale Yarborough hung up his helmet late in the decade and became the owner of his own team, and Alan Kulwicki, an engineer, brought his American Speed Association titles and talent with him as he moved to NASCAR from his native Wisconsin and started his team as both owner and driver. Robert Yates, a top engine builder and mechanic, hocked all he had to buy out Harry Rainer and assembled his own team with Davey Allison as his first driver. The late 1980s also saw sports car owner Jack Roush come to stock car racing with Mark Martin as his driver. New Jersey highway builders Bill and Mickey Stavola came to the sport and picked up Bobby Hillin, Jr, to drive. They won at Talladega and soon started fielding a second car with Bobby Allison as the driver. Allison was in their car when he suffered career-ending injuries in a first-lap crash at Pocono in 1988.

Allison was one of the old guard who concluded their driving careers during the 1980s. David Pearson and Yarborough had both retired, as had Benny Parsons and Buddy Baker.

There were new faces and new places for them to be seen in the decade. When the southern California road course at Riverside gave way to industrial development in 1987, the track's two dates were split. One went to the Sears Point Raceway in northern California and the other to the mile oval at Phoenix. In 1986 the circuit also returned, after a two-decade hiatus, to the famed Watkins Glen circuit in upstate New York.

The racing machines had changed, too. From the totally stock cars of the 1949 season, the machines became purpose-built engineering marvels which used only a few factory parts. Outwardly they resembled their street brothers, but under the sleek, massaged, aerodynamic exteriors they were now pure racing machines able to reach and maintain high speed yet protect the driver when they crashed at those speeds.

The decade saw Richard Petty win his 200th and final race. It came at Daytona on July 4th, 1984 and his victory record is likely never to be matched in the future. (A rookie driver starting now would have to win every race for six years to get within striking distance of that number.) Among those in attendance for Petty's milestone was Ronald Reagan, president of the United States, who had given the command to "Start Your Engines" from Air Force One en route to the track.

As the 1980s ended, tracks were building grandstands at every opportunity to accommodate the ever-growing requests for tickets to their Winston Cup events.

The 1990s

The upward spiral of the sport's popularity was not only climbing, it was doing so at an ever-accelerating rate as the 1990s came on the horizon.

As the stock car racing under the NASCAR banner sped into the final years of its first half century the expansion and growth were phenomenal. New areas welcomed the sport. New divisions were created and existing ones given more strength and support. New stars zoomed into its galaxy. More money poured in. New champions were crowned. Multi-car teams returned. And the NASCAR name itself became prominent at the places away from the race tracks. But the period was not without sadness. Two of its brightest young stars were lost, a king retired, another of the sport's original facilities closed and the founder passed away during the 1990s.

For nearly three decades the sport's expansion had come via going to tracks built for other kinds of racing or adding events at already existing facilities, places like Pocono, Sears Point and Phoenix. In the 1990s, however, facilities were being built with the intent of hosting NASCAR's Winston Cup and other divisions specifically. New Hampshire International

Speedway, a mile oval at Loudon, was the first and opened the sport to the New England area including nearby Boston. In 1997 Texas Motor Speedway at Fort Worth, a mile-and-a-half track similar in design to Charlotte, saw the sport return to the Lone Star State after an absence of nearly two decades and the same year a two-mile tri-oval which aped the Michigan design emerged at Fontana as Roger Penske's California Speedway gave southern California a showcase for NASCAR racing which had been missing since the close of the state's tracks at Riverside and Ontario in the 1980s.

The largest addition came in the middle of the decade when NASCAR's major league made their first venture onto the hallowed two-and-a-half rectangular track

at Indianapolis. It was a move the Indianapolis purist abhorred but one the track and race fans adored as more than 300,000 poured out to watch history made as the stock car roared and raced where previously only the sleek open-wheeled "Champ cars"

NASCAR expands towards the 21st century

had competed. The race, called the "Brickyard 400", immediately became not only the biggest-attended event in the sport's history, it was also the richest with more than $3 million in posted awards. The race saw inaugural winner Jeff Gordon, in just his second season of Winston Cup competition, pick up a record $613,000. His winnings in that race alone were more than pioneers like Lee Petty, Ned Jarrett and Junior Johnson won in their careers.

Another new track, this one a mile-and-a-half tri-oval in Las Vegas, joined the NASCAR ranks in early 1998 with Mark Martin the inaugural winner in a Jack Roush Ford. Meanwhile all existing tracks were adding thousands of seats as ticket demand for their Winston Cup races continued to far exceed the number of seats available.

With the skyrocketing growth came change, too. To make room for events at new tracks, some of the old ones had to be discarded. Bruton Smith bought half interest in the track at North Wilkesboro, North Carolina, in order to secure a date for his new Texas facility. Bob Bahre wanted a second event at his new facility in New Hampshire and purchased the other half of the North Carolina oval, one of the 1948 original NASCAR tracks. Each moved one of the North Wilkesboro dates to their facility and the track was left idle. Ironically the winner of the 1996 final race at the historic site was young Jeff Gordon, who was born the year the track had celebrated its 23rd year of hosting NASCAR races.

Gordon, a native of northern California who had moved to Indiana as a youth to continue a career in midgets and sprint cars before heading to the NASCAR ranks early in the decade, was just one of the fresh faces in the sport. He joined the youth movement in the period which saw Terry Labonte's younger brother Bobby follow in his older sibling's tiretracks, the Burton brothers—Jeff and Ward—Alan Kulwicki and Johnny Benson from the ASA ranks and John Andretti from Indy cars, as well as a number of drivers from the Busch Grand National ranks, all moved into stock car racing's big league. Their arrival filled the gaps left by retirements of drivers like Bobby Allison, Cale Yarborough, Buddy Baker and Benny Parsons, as well as the loss of 1992 champion Kulwicki and the popular Davey Allison in aircraft accidents in 1993.

While the teams gathered in June for their 1992 race at Sears Point, word came that Bill France, Sr, the founder of NASCAR and builder of the tracks at Daytona and Talladega, had died after a long battle with age-related disease. It was a sad time for the sport he had founded and led until he turned the organization's presidency over to his son two decades earlier.

But the sport continued and came to the season's conclusion at Atlanta in November. It was a race which found six drivers with a shot at the championship and marked the end of an era. It was the race where the sport's unofficial king, Richard Petty, was scheduled to make the final start of his 200-victory, seven-championship career that covered more than a third of a century. It was also where a newcomer made his first start after a successful stint in the Busch ranks, an arrival little noticed with the point battle and Petty's finale as Jeff Gordon drove a Winston Cup car into the sport's major league.

Petty was involved in an earlier accident, but his crew salvaged the day by repairing the car so "The King" could be running at the finish of his final event. All the point contenders encountered trouble except for Kulwicki and Bill Elliott. They dueled throughout the race. Kulwicki led one more lap than race winner Elliott to pick up the points needed to take the title. It came with nine to spare as he took the crown by ten, the closest margin in history.

Other NASCAR divisions were changing, too. In the early 1980s NASCAR had taken the Late Model Sportsman division and made it the Busch Grand National Series with a national tour of its own which began holding events west of the Mississippi late in the 1990s. In the midst of the 1970s the sanctioning organization had seen the growth in sub-compact cars on the streets and highways and formed the Goody's Dash series for those vehicles.

Similarly, in the middle of the '90s, NASCAR noted the growing popularity of pickup trucks around the country. By 1994 plans were afoot to start a racing division for them. It became a reality in 1995 and has become one of the fastest growing divisions in the sanctioning body's history. Other divisions prospered in the 1990s with regional weekly short-track competitors battling for divisional and national championships in the Winston Racing Series and a dirt-track circuit in the midwest, tours in the Northwest, modifieds in the Northeast and competition in all four quadrants of the nation.

The '90s saw every Winston Cup race televised live and the same for the Busch Series and Truck events. Track revenues soared and the race teams benefited. In NASCAR's 50th season, 1997, every Winston Cup race offered posted awards for their events in excess of a million dollars. Some were worth two or three times that amount. The post-season point fund grew accordingly. The Winston Cup fund, which began at $100,000 in 1971, had swelled to $13 million in 2001. When Jeff Gordon won the 2001 title he walked off the stage in New York's banquet with more than four million dollars in post-season awards to go with the $6.5 million he had won during the 36-race season. It was a far cry from the $1,000 Red Byron got as the division's first champion in 1949.

Another change came as the 1990s moved along. Owners fielding multi-car teams—Junior Johnson, Petty Engineering and the Wood brothers—had shown up with two car efforts in the '60s, '70s or '80s, but in the 1990s there were the pairs and even trios. Rick Hendrick had two full-time teams and added a third as the decade progressed. He was soon joined by Cuban emigré Felix Sabates who had three cars at every event. They were all topped by Jack Roush who began with a single car and as NASCAR's age passed 50 years had swelled that number to five. By the end of the 2001 campaign over half of a 43-car field could consist of cars racing against another machine from the same stable.

The growing popularity of NASCAR racing was reflected by its attraction of people from other pro sports. NBA star Brad Daugherty was among the first as he became half owner of a NASCAR Busch team and later a Craftsman

Truck entry. He was soon followed by former NFL player and coach Jerry Glanville who raced in both Busch and Truck competition. Pro football was a loser when former Superbowl winning coach of the Washington Redskins Joe Gibbs left the sport to become the owner of a Winston Cup team. Mark Rypien, one of Gibbs' MVP superbowl quarterbacks, was part owner of a Busch Team with his former college classmate Chad Little as driver. Also a group of major league baseball players were co-owners of a Busch team driven by Bobby Hillin and Miami Dolphins quarterback Dan Marino became co-owner of Bill Elliott's second Winston Cup team for driver Jerry Nadeau.

Bill France, Jr. carries on his father's dream.

The decade saw NASCAR expand in other areas. In 1996 they took many of the top teams to Japan for an exhibition race and branched out with retail stores and NASCAR cafes as the popularity soared on its continuing upward climb. Tracks expanded their gift shops and Daytona Speedway added an interactive tourist attraction, "Daytona USA", where fans could learn more about the sport and the rich heritage of racing. Much of the latter expansions came from the continuation of the France family. Bill France, Jr.'s children, son Brian and daughter Lesa, had moved into responsible positions in NASCAR and the speedway, respectively. Brian France, who became the NASCAR executive vice president, brought about the opening of a NASCAR office in New York, led the move to NASCAR-themed stores and dining establishments while also overseeing the licensing of the NASCAR name for souvenir sales. Lesa France Kennedy, vice executive of International speedway corporation, was the creator of the motorsports-themed attraction which opened as a tribute to her grandparents, Bill and Anne France, Sr, and draws thousands of visitors year round.

As the decade of the '90s closed the sport was solid. A new, lucrative television pact was in place that afforded all Winston Cup races being shown live, post-season point funds were in excess of $13 million and there was a newness in tracks and faces in victory lanes as well as at the top of the sanctioning body. Bill France, Junior turned over the presidency of the organization to Mike Helton in November 2000. It marked the first time in the organization's history it had not been headed by someone named France. The decade had seen new facilities in New Hampshire, California, Texas, Nevada and south Florida. Jeff Gordon, Bobby Labonte, the Burton brothers – Jeff and Ward, Tony Stewart and Dale Earnhardt, Jr. all emerged among the new winners in the sport's biggest league.

As the world entered the new millennium NASCAR's 2001 schedule was its most ambitious and lucrative. A grueling 36-race slate awaited the competitors with events at new tracks in Illinois and Kansas, all of them shown on the new television package that attracted record viewers. The gleaming promise of the new was overshadowed quickly. The first race of 2001, the 43rd annual Daytona 500, saw super star Dale Earnhardt fatally injured on the final lap. The seven-time series champion, all-time top money winner in motorsports and winningest driver in Daytona history became the first death in that race (or the 400-mile July event there) and the 29th in the division's 53 year history covering all the testing, practice, qualifying and racing on all of the 168 different tracks where it has competed. Although grieving, the sport moved on with new drivers adding their names to the list of those who had won in the highly competitive world of NASCAR.

NASCAR and stock car racing have come literally thousands of miles since Bill France, Sr, got a small group together at a Daytona Beach hotel in 1947. Most of those miles were uphill and many were bumpy, but they have taken the sport across the country and overseas. They have made many people wealthy and caused the athletes to become household names. Even the tall former auto mechanic's brilliant foresight could not have envisioned the heights his sport would achieve in the first 50 years. The best may be yet to come.

The Driving Force Behind NASCAR

NASCAR is as much a family sport as it is about the machinery and the science of cars. One family has been at the helm of the sport since its conception in 1948—the France family.

Cold hands, an unaccepted 15-cent collect call and extraordinary foresight were the ingredients which led a tall mechanic from America's capital on a path of unmatched success in auto racing and the founding of a family dynasty.

William Henry Getty France was born to a farming couple in 1909. He learned a strong work ethic as he grew up doing the chores on the small family farm near Washington, D.C., where hard work was a way of life. He also learned how to fix the machines when they broke, which was often. The latter work enthralled young Bill France for it taught him how and why machines worked, what made them tick and thump. He enjoyed fixing things.

As a teenager his mechanical bent drew him to the nearby mile-and-a-quarter board track at Laurel, Maryland. He was awed as the speedy

Duesenbergs flew around the steeply banked oval. He also was able to sneak the family car, a model T, onto the track and turn a few laps himself. It whetted a deep-seated appetite for racing in the youngster, but created problems when he had to mask his emotions and stifle a laugh as he went to the local tire store and complained about their tires being worn out so quickly.

His mechanical skills stood him in good stead when he went in search of work after his high school days. He

was quickly hired at a local garage. He enjoyed all the facets of fixing and tuning up cars except one. During the area's cold winters, cars were balky and often wouldn't start in the mornings. The strapping young mechanic, now well over six feet tall and powerfully built by the farm labors, was the one sent to assist the customers in getting their automobiles cranked up. It was chilling work and became a time of year he dreaded.

The summers he didn't mind. In his spare time he had built an open-wheeled race car similar to a midget. It had a wooden frame and the body was covered with canvas. He even built the engine. With his car he raced at a dirt track at Pikeville, Maryland. He was good at his vocation, but years later wondered why his primitive machine never caught fire

and burned up.

Bill France, now a wage-earning 20 year old, met a young nurse named Anne Bledsoe from Nathans Creek, North Carolina, who was working in the Washington area. They courted and were married in 1931. Their first child, William Clifton France, was born three years later.

The winter of 1933 had been especially cold. France decided that if he was to be a mechanic, he might as well be one in a warmer climate, like Florida. At least there his fingers would not feel frozen during the months of short daylight. France decided to take his young family and move south.

With $25 in his pocket and three times that amount in the bank account, France loaded up his tools, put Anne and little Bill Junior in their Hupmobile and, towing a small trailer packed with their meager possessions and his little race car, they headed for warm and sunny Florida.

A long-standing myth has the car breaking down near Daytona as they headed for Miami. It is a story France had to debunk frequently. "We stopped in Daytona because we had decided we wanted to live there," France would relate. "I was a pretty good mechanic. If the car had broken down, I could have fixed it and gone on."

He was a mechanic and had little trouble finding work at a local auto dealership. He and Anne soon had a small home on the city's peninsula not too far from the hard-packed sands of the beach. France was well aware of the area's renown as a center of speed, a reputation built on the speed runs which had been held there since 1902. The association with racing was one of the draws which had brought the young family to settle there.

When 1935 arrived, France had bought a small gasoline station on Main Street in Daytona, a structure with a work bay where he could work on customers' cars. It was from that locale he ventured to watch England's Sir Malcolm Campbell take his powerful Bluebird to a world's land speed record of 276-plus miles-an-hour average in his two-way run through the measured mile on the southerly end of the long, white beach. What France and the other spectators did not know as they watched the history-making endeavor was that it would be the last such mark established on the beach. The strip of sand along the Atlantic Ocean was subject to the whims of the tides and wind. The speedsters had located a long salt lake in Utah where the surface was more constant.

After the 1935 record the land speed tries were moved to Bonneville's salt flats in Utah where speeds have since elevated above the 600 mile-an-hour mark.

Their departure left Daytona's civic officials in a quandary about how to maintain the area's reputation as a racing center and keep the winter tourists returning. They settled on a stock car race for the winter of 1936. It would be held on a course of a mile and a half of the beach and an equal distance of the parallel Highway A1A. The two straightaways would be joined by a pair of tight horseshoe turns at either end. (The southern end of that course sits now at the Dunlawton Avenue beach approach in South Daytona. The North Turn lies under high rise condominiums.) The 1936 race was put on and promoted by the city. It attracted an all-star cast of characters. "Mad Milt" Marion from Canada, "Wild Bill" Cummings the 1934 Indy 500 winner, "Doc" MacKenzie who was the prior year's AAA dirt track champ, Bob Sall the 1933 Eastern AAA champion, Major Goldie Gardner of England and a local mechanic named Bill France.

There were Fords aplenty in the field as well as Auburns, an Oldsmobile, a Chevrolet, a couple of Willys, a Dodge and a Lincoln Zephyr. Mad Milt Marion drove his Ford to victory in the 240-mile race that took over four-and-a-half hours to complete. Coming home fifth was France, who had also turned the wrenches on Marion's winning machine.

The race was a fiasco. The heavy cars ground the turns into sandy hog wallows. Cars stalled and became obstacles in both turns and on the straights. To top it all the city officials claimed to have lost $22,000 on the event. They went out of the race promotion business and were replaced by the local Elks Club for the 1937 effort which was won by Carl "Smokey" Purser of Daytona. France ran again but didn't finish as the Elks lost money on the project supported mostly with their name and not much in funding.

Plans for a 1938 event were stymied by lack of sponsorship. The local Chamber of Commerce came to France, aware of his driving and racing knowledge, to enlist his assistance in finding a promoter. France tried to make a collect telephone call to one he knew.

The man, unnamed to this day, declined to accept the 15 cent charge.

Lamenting the turn-down with his friend and local restaurant owner Charlie Reese, the two discussed the potential loss of racing to the area. Reese pointed out France's many contacts with drivers and car owners and his knowledge of the promotions which had worked at other venues. Reese owned Charlie's Grill and Hi-Hat Club, a profitable Seabreeze Boulevard restaurant and night club in Daytona, and agreed to post the prize money if France would organize the race and get the cars and drivers.

The discussion created the Daytona Beach Racing Association. Reese put up the money and France handled all the leg work. It was the beginning of Bill France's career as a race promoter although he would continue driving and he, with side-by-side help from Anne, still operated their gas station.

The first promotional effort was a small success. The race was won by Danny Murphy with France finishing second. (Fourth place that July day in 1938 was a peanut farmer from South Carolina named Harold Brasington. The lanky Brasington would later build a big paved track at Darlington, South Carolina where a new organization called "NASCAR" would hold a 500-mile race for stock cars in 1950. He would also be instrumental in the creation of the North Carolina Speedway at Rockingham in the mid-1960s.)

After paying the purse, lap prizes and reimbursing the City for its assistance, France and Reese split the profit of $200.

Bolstered by that small measure of success France continued racing, mechanicking and promoting. He performed the second of those tasks in May at a brick covered track in Indiana where he twisted wrenches for Joel Thorne, the ninth place finisher in the 1938 Indianapolis 500.

Bill France to the fore

France's driving and promotional skills continued to grow. The 1939 and 1940 Daytona races were bigger and better than the year before. France himself drove the winning car in the 1940 event and went on to be acclaimed the Stock Car Racing champion after a haphazard season which saw him win often but without any kind of point system or national organization.

Along his way France mentally noted the many foibles of his sport. Unscrupulous promoters who ducked out before paying the advertised prize money. A lack of safety or technical rules. Unsafe spectator areas. A deficit of media coverage in local papers or on radio. No insurance to cover drivers or mechanics injured in competition. He felt these conditions were not right and vowed to correct them if and when he had the chance.

After the 1941 races, and there were three that year on the beach course, all motorsports came to an abrupt halt with America's entry into World War Two following the bombing of Pearl Harbor on December 7.

During the war years France's mechanical skills were expended at the Daytona Boatworks building submarine chasers while Anne minded the Main Street garage and gave birth to their second child, James C. "Jimmy" France, in 1944.

With the cessation of hostilities in 1945 and the returning of the soldiers, airmen, sailors and marines, racing was ready to resume and France was ready to help it.

The first post-war race in Daytona ran April 14, 1946 and was promoted by France, who also ran fourth in the event won by Alabama's Robert "Red" Byron. Byron, a wounded Air Force sergeant who had raced in some of France's pre-war events, who would play a significant role in his future, also.

France retired from driving after that season. He saw the future held more promise with him on the promotional

and organizational side of the sport rather than behind the steering wheel of a race car. While the year was France's last as a race driver, it was the starting year for his eldest son, Bill Junior, who got into the racing business by selling programs, vending at concession stands, selling or stubbing tickets and other chores which would help a race occur.

The father and son, the latter now in his early teens, worked together during the 1947 races with the youngster also attending Seabreeze High School in Daytona during the school year, but traveling with his parents to races at other times. Anne handled the books and wrote the checks while Bill and Billy were all over the tracks.

Toward the end of the year, as the racing season wound down, France recalled the problems he had become aware of while racing before the war. Maybe, he thought, now is the time to do something about them. He decided to assemble a meeting that December in Daytona and discuss the problems with others who shared his interest in stock car racing.

The meeting was held in Daytona Beach at the Streamline Hotel. Some 35 men—drivers, mechanics, bootleggers and businessmen—attended. The three-day gathering resulted with the formation of the National Association for Stock Car Auto Racing—NASCAR.

Now with uniform rules, a point system, insurance for competitors and assurance of prize money payment, stock car racing was on its way to becoming a national sport.

Red Byron won the first NASCAR race in February 1948 and would go on to win its first championship. The following season France's old on-track rival was also the champion on the new car "Strictly Stock" circuit which became the Winston Cup Series of future years.

The France family worked long and hard together to make the concept grow. Bill Sr ran the organization and promoted races with Anne, by now an excellent business-woman, keeping check on the money flow and Bill Jr doing whatever tasks he was assigned. He flagged, drove motor graders, stapled advertising posters to barns and telephone poles, parked cars and sold tickets. He even drove race cars a few times, but quickly learned he was better suited behind the scenes. Mostly, though, he learned the business of auto racing and, as the future has proven, he learned well.

Through the family's sacrifice and dedication to the sport it grew and prospered. Under Bill France's leadership the sport spread across the country. As Jimmy grew he, too, was swept into the family's efforts.

Taking NASCAR one step further

In the early 1950s Bill Senior could see the encroaching development along the beach-road cours. He recalled the big crowds and magnificence of the races at Indianapolis in the 1930s. He thought of having a similar track for his sport, only he wanted it better and faster. His plans for such a facility began in 1953, but would take a half dozen years to gather support, engineering and financing to make them into a reality. Meanwhile he continued building the sport by talking, cajoling, twisting arms and shaking hands. He employed his warm personality or his stern taskmaster approach as a situation might dictate. He could be a charmer or a czar, but he got it done.

The geographic spread of his sport required almost continuous travel. He quickly realized he needed to be flying from place to place rather than losing so many hours driving. He learned to fly, a skill that called on many of the abilities which had made him a good race driver, and was soon piloting himself around the country in his own airplane. (Many years later NASCAR would have a fleet of aircraft including several jets.)

In 1959 France's second dream came to fruition as he opened the high banked, two-and-a-half mile Daytona International Speedway on a site that had been a cypress swamp just west of Daytona Beach. The track's first big race, the Daytona 500, was a whopping success with Lee Petty and Johnny Beauchamp taking the checkered flag in a photo-finish. After three days of studying news photos, Petty was declared the winner—by inches.

The whole family had been involved in the track's construction and the presentation of the event. France Sr and Jr had worked with contractors, driven equipment, sold shares of stock, built and overseen the endeavor. Anne supervised the ticket office and handled the book-keeping in addition to her duties as treasurer of NASCAR. Even Jim, now 15, was put to work in the mailing room, in the parking lots or assisting his parents and older brother. He stayed in his preferred shadows of the business of racing as an officer and official of the sanctioning body and the track, quietly making things happen. Both NASCAR and the Speedway are family efforts.

The Frances continued to work and were now aided by sizeable staffs as both projects continued to grow. But Bill Sr, never content with the status quo, had another idea. He would build another track, even bigger and faster than his Daytona showplace.

With his vision and ability to get things done, coupled with Anne's finger on the purse strings, Talladega Speedway opened in Alabama just a decade after the Daytona facility. It was one of four big new tracks which joined the NASCAR circuit during the 1969 season. Those additions showed everyone the strength and growth of stock car racing under France's direction.

In the early 1970s France made a decisive move by convincing the R. J. Reynolds Tobacco giant, through their Winston brand, to join the sport as the major sponsor of the Grand National circuit, the biggest of NASCAR's many divisions, which would become the Winston Cup Series. Lending the corporate's expertise in marketing and promotional skills to the glamour and excitement of the new car competition was the cornerstone of national expansion.

Passing the reins from father to son

After a quarter of a century of leading the sport he founded, Bill France announced in early 1972 he was stepping down as the only president NASCAR had known. The reins he had held so tightly for so long would be entrusted to the capable hands of his son and co-worker, Bill Jr. It was quickly apparent the son had also inherited his father's work ethic and conservative approach. Both believed in being slow to make changes. Options were considered and alternatives mulled over. It was a slow and, to some, aggravating process, but a way of doing things which proved correct over the years.

Without skipping a beat both enterprises continued to flourish. Bill Jr bolstered the weekly NASCAR tracks, broadened the scope of the sport by creating a division for the popular sub-compacts, had better point systems developed, sought new arenas for NASCAR racing and attracted Fortune 500 companies to stock car racing. He refined and developed what his father had created. He withstood challenges with the same skill and aplomb. He had also married—a former track beauty queen—and he and Betty Jane were soon parents of a son and daughter.

Whereas Bill France, Jr, has obtained his business acumen from his parents and through the school of hard knocks, he made certain his children went to college. Both graduated with an emphasis on the business and marketing aspects of sports.

As NASCAR and International Speedway Corporation moved into the 1990s, the third generation of the France family was heavily involved. Bill Sr's grandson, Bill's son Brian, is NASCAR senior vice president and directs marketing and communications. It was his idea to expand the NASCAR offices to New York, Charlotte and California, to create a racing division for the popular pick-up trucks, and to broaden the NASCAR horizon with retail souvenir shops and racing-themed cafes away from race tracks. The daughter, Lesa France Kennedy, directs growth and strategic planning for both the speedway empire that now includes Daytona, Talladega, Watkins Glen, Darlington, Phoenix, Kansas City and several more.

Both Brian and Lesa learned the way their father did—by doing. Brian worked in all phases of NASCAR from inspecting cars at short tracks to running a weekly oval in Arizona. He, too, has picked up trash, directed traffic, flagged and sold tickets. His sister, now married to a Daytona physician, learned the business side of the sport working alongside her grandmother in the accounting and ticket counters of the race tracks. It was at the latter she learned the family's great priority on customer service. The granddaughter of the NASCAR and Daytona Speedway founder came up with the concept for the successful "Daytona USA" racing-themed interactive attraction located at the Florida's speedway entrance. Wearing her NASCAR hat, Lesa is also charged with the impossible task of phasing new tracks into the circuit.

After over 60 years of marriage and the founding of a racing empire and dynasty, Anne France died in January 1992. Five months later Bill France, Sr, also died. Their passing was mourned by thousands. Friends and even admiring foes understood the contributions they had made to their community and to the nation's sports environment. They left behind the most successful racing organization in history and left it in able family hands.

Due to the load imposed by the growth and expansion of the sport and widening circle of ISC tracks, Bill France, Junior turned over the day-to-day NASCAR operations to trusted aid Mike Helton in February 1999. A battle with cancer sapped his strength and diverted his focus causing France to name Helton NASCAR's new President in November 2000. After a 53-year run, 29 of them under his direction, Bill France moved to the newly created position of Chairman of the Board and relinquished to presidency of NASCAR to someone whose surname was not "France".

NASCAR and International Speedway Corporation have become multi-million dollar enterprises. All because Bill France didn't like the cold winters in Washington, D.C., because a race promoter would not accept a 15-cent collect call and because the tall farmer's son could not only see the future, but made it happen.

Periodically, every enterprise evaluates its progress. As **NASCAR** concluded its first half century of racing it asked an elite panel of veteran observers to pick the best they had seen during that span of time. Their choices make up the following pages.

Red Byron

The man who was NASCAR's first winner

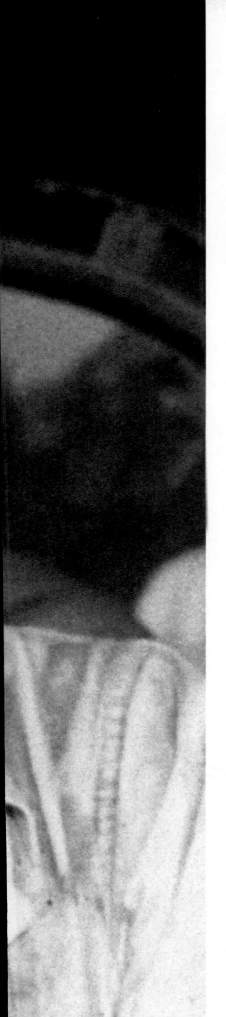

He was smooth and consistent when he needed to drive that way, but could be bold and daring when victory was in sight.

His success during 1948's inaugural NASCAR season lay, in part, in his skill behind the wheel of cars—mostly 1939 Ford coupes owned by Atlanta's Raymond Parks and tuned by Jerome "Red" Vogt—and his fearless nature. He had just returned from flying through the valley of death in the war.

When NASCAR ran its first race, on the silver sands and on the narrow asphalt highway which paralleled the beach in 1948, it was Byron who emerged the first-ever winner under the sanctioning body's banner. It was a season which saw him win eleven more times in the 52 races and earn sufficient points to become the first driving

> ## "Red was an extra good driver. He'd get going about half way through the race. I think he'd stack up fine to this day. Red was very smart, very shrewd ... very hard to beat."
> ### Raymond Parks

champion. Included on his 1948 victory list was one at Richmond, Virginia, on the site where the sanctioning body still races half a century later.

With the 1949 organization of a new car division, it was again the Byron-Parks-Vogt combination which won two of the eight races and amassed four top five finishes in just six starts to become the division's inaugural champion. Byron was the division's first winner at the half-mile oval at Martinsville, Virginia, another of the current venues.

The next season he was second in the season opener on the beach course at Daytona and with the advent of the first superspeedway event—Darlington in 1950—it was Byron driving Parks' Oldsmobile to a third place finish, despite never having raced on a paved track.

Byron, who died of a heart attack in 1960 while managing a sports car team, ran just four years in NASCAR competition, but the skills displayed and titles earned made him a sure shot for inclusion among the sport's all-time greats.

Winner of the Modified Division in 1948 and the Winston Cup in 1949

Marshall Teague, a Daytona Beach native, was not only an outstanding race car driver, he was also an outstanding mechanic and had a good business sense. It was an odd combination for a racing car star in the formative years of stock car racing.

An Air Force flight engineer who flew the Burma "Hump" during World War Two, Teague returned to his hometown after the war and used his military pay to buy a Pure Oil gas station. He also got back to racing, a sport he had watched while growing up and attending Seabreeze High School in the city before the military days.

Teague was at the 1947 organizational meeting which formed NASCAR and was elected its first

Marshall Teague

NASCAR's first treasurer

Treasurer. But it was his dazzling driving style which got him included among these 50 top talents.

When he built and drove his Hudson Hornet to victory in the 1951 beach-road course race, it created a problem for NASCAR. They did not have the manufacturer's specifications for the car to determine its compliance with the stock car rules. The executives at Hudson learned of the win when NASCAR called to request information. The Hudson officials invited Teague and his wife to Detroit in recognition. Teague so impressed the company brass they agreed to supply him with cars and parts. Resulting publicity let Pure Oil executives know one of their dealers had won a big race in Florida so they, too, invited Teague to the firm's Illinois offices where Teague induced them into supplying fuel and lubricants for the races. That 1951 trip created the first factory support by a car maker and the first contingency program by an accessory company. Both were achieved by Teague's style and presence.

Teague and his wife drove the two new Hornets they had been given back to Florida and Teague picked North Carolina driver, Herb Thomas, to drive the second car in the 1951 Darlington 500-miler. Thomas qualified second in the 82-car field. Teague, who spent most of his time getting Thomas' car ready, didn't earn his 42nd place berth until posting the quickest time of the event later in the qualifying. But it was Teague who thrilled the crowd as he sailed through the field to take the lead by the 13th lap. Thomas went on to win after Teague's mount was sidelined by a wreck.

Teague won the beach race again in 1952 with Thomas bringing the other "Teaguemobile" Hudson home in second. It was also a one-two punch delivered by the duo in the following week's race at Jacksonville, Florida.

The first driver to get factory support from a manufacturer after his 1951 win at Daytona

Although he ran just four years under the NASCAR banner, Teague won seven of his 23 races. He led nearly half of the laps he finished and later was the first driver to take the Indy 500 Rookie test without a year of open-wheel racing experience.

He perished while racing at Daytona Speedway while testing an Indy car just a few days before the first Daytona 500 was held in 1959.

Few men, if any, have done so much in stock car racing in such a short period as the thin, hawk-nosed farmer from Sanford, NC, named Herb Thomas.

He was part of the tour in 1949, running just four of the eight events. The first season he won the first of his 48 races. Before injuries forced his retirement six years later, he had become the first driver to win two championships in the major league of stock car racing and was the first to win the circuit's only 500-mile race three times. The latter feat included the first back-to-back triumph in the prestigious event in 1954 and 1955. The consecutive wins are even more astounding since he had been seriously injured in a racing accident just three months prior to the second triumph.

Herbert W. Thomas won in a variety of car makes, for several owners and on both dirt and asphalt tracks.

Herb Thomas

1954 and '55 winner of Daytona 500

His greatest success came at the wheel of his own cars and in the potent Chryslers fielded by the irascible Carl Keikhaefer. His best season came in 1953 when he started 37 races with a dozen wins, eight seconds, seven more top fives and another four in the top 10. That year he had 31 of 37 race results in the top 10 and also won 10 poles *en route* to his second championship.

He might well have won a third. Leading the points race late in the 1956 campaign, Thomas was seriously injured in a late-season accident in a hastily

First to win two championships in the major league

scheduled race at Shelby, NC. The wreck and severity of injuries all but ended the popular driver's career and deprived him of becoming his sport's first three-time champion.

When he finally hung up his helmet, he left a record of 48 wins and 38 poles in 230 races. His winning percentage of 20.97 per cent still ranks best among all of the series champions in 49 seasons.

Thomas was able to attend the 1998 Daytona 500 to be recognized as one of the sport's 50 greatest drivers. He was the earliest former champion on hand as he returned 47 years after taking the first title. Thomas passed away in August 2000 at age 77.

Tall, handsome, blond Curtis Morton Turner was part of the NASCAR scene from the start. Once called "The Babe Ruth of Stock Car Racing" by *Sports Illustrated*, his flamboyant style off the track was as eye catching as his skill in handling a broadsliding car around a dirt track.

He was one of the 14 drivers to win during the 52-race 1948 inaugural season for NASCAR racing when he was the first to the checkered flag seven times. He was the fourth to win when the "Strictly Stock" new car division was introduced the following year. His first triumph in the new class came at the circular one-mile Langhorne, Pennsylvania track in an Olds 88 on

Curtis Turner

Race-winner in the inaugural season

August 11, the fourth race of the division's history. Sixteen years later, after most of his earlier contemporaries had retired, he scored his 17th and final victory in the inaugural event at North Carolina Motor Speedway, a 500-mile speed and endurance contest on a one-mile track.

Between those two, he scored too in other NASCAR divisions—Modified, Sportsman and Convertible.

Subscribing to the philosophy, "Run it 'til it breaks or wins," Turner led the major league in 1950s laps completed, laps led and races led, although he won just four of his 16 starts.

A businessman who bought and sold tracts of timber, Turner was among the first drivers who flew their own airplanes to distant races, and was instrumental in convincing NASCAR founder Bill France to learn to fly.

Noted for his affinity for hosting parties, Turner once drove and won a race in all but the coat of a handsome silver silk suit at Columbia, SC, Speedway, but he did loosen the tie.

Turner was banned from the sport for attempting to organize the

drivers into a union in the early 1960s. During the suspension, he lost several years when he might have extended his victory list. During the late 1950s, Turner was the terror of NASCAR's Convertible division, boasting 38 wins in the series' 117 events.

The Roanoke, Virginia native lost his life in an airplane accident in October 1970, but has been voted into several racing Halls of Fame for the driving skills he displayed, which earned him a rightful place among the sport's elite 50.

Led the major league statistics in the 1950s in terms of laps completed, laps led and races led

The transition was easy for Elzie Wylie Baker. He merely changed vehicles when he gave up his job as a city bus driver to become one of the greatest stock car chauffeurs of all time. Well, he allows that maybe he was not that good as a bus driver. He might park his big vehicle at the end of his route—and near his race shop—and spend a while tinkering with his car.

Like many of the pioneers who made it onto the all-time list of greats of stock car racing, Baker was there, rubbing fenders and broadsliding on the dirt track under the new NASCAR banner

Buck Baker

46-time winner in 25-year career

in 1948. He was there, too, when the new car division was inaugurated on the three-quarter mile track in his North Carolina hometown on June 19, 1949. Behind the steering wheel of a 1948 Kaiser, he bumped through the rutted turns and ate the swirling red dust on his way to an 11th-place finish.

He didn't win that season, nor the next. His breakthrough came early in the 1952 campaign, when he piloted a Hudson Hornet to victory in a 200-lap event on a half-mile track in Columbia, SC. That would be the first of 46 triumphs in a 25-year career in the sport's major league—a driving stint which also saw him the top qualifier in 44 races.

The first back-to-back winner in the Winston Cup championship (1956 and 1957)—and in two different makes of car

Buck Baker was the first back-to-back champion in the division now known as Winston Cup and won them in different makes of car to indicate the driver, not the machine, was the deciding factor. He took the title for the first time in 1956 and repeated the feat the following season. For three straight years (1955–57), Baker was the top lap and mileage driver. His victory list includes three in the venerable Southern 500 race at Darlington, the circuit's first and oldest race at the classic 500-mile duration.

Baker also gave to the sport. He passed his skills onto his son, Buddy (who is also listed in this special 50). Also, since retiring from competition in the early 1970s he has taught hundreds of hopeful, future Buck or Buddy Bakers the art of stock car racing at his driving schools at North Carolina Speedway and Georgia's Atlanta Motor Speedway.

Lee Petty

The first three-time winner of Winston Cup

the help of attrition, he moved up as the dusty day progressed. Running well at the half-way mark of the 200 laps, the Buick's wheel caught a rut and flipped. Over and over it tumbled before coming to rest, badly wrinkled, on all four wheels. Dejected, Petty climbed from his mashed machine and sat on the upper rim of the third turn pondering how he would get himself and his boys home and, more importantly, how he would explain the damage to the family's sedan to his wife waiting at home.

Petty wasn't discouraged, merely challenged. He had enjoyed the competition and was capable of running with the regular racers. He wanted more. He ran five of the seven remaining races in that 1949 season and earned his first victory that fall on the half-mile dirt track Heidelberg Speedway near Pittsburgh. His runs were good enough to find his name second on the year's point standings at season's end. It was a list he would top three times before a crash through the guard rail in a qualifying race at Daytona in 1961 resulted in injuries which all but ended his brilliant career.

The "founder" of a NASCAR dynasty

Always smooth and steady on the track, detailed and thorough in preparation of his machines, Lee Petty began a dynasty in the sport which saw his son Richard become a seven-time champion and score a record 200 victories in a brilliant career. His grandson Kyle Petty (Richard's son) also became a winner in the division he helped found and emerged from as one of the great stars of the circuit which has become Winston Cup racing. Petty, 85, died in March 2000, just a month before his great grandson Adam became the fourth generation of the family to start a Winston Cup race.

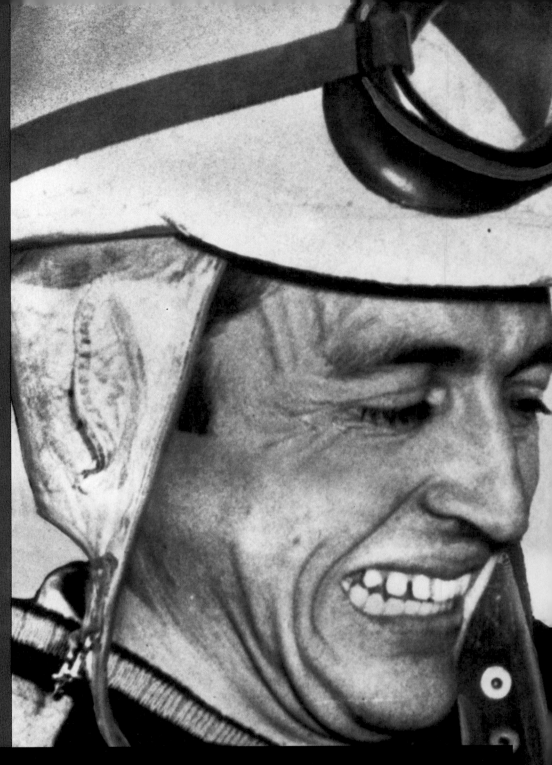

The youngest of the famed racing brothers from Fort Payne, Alabama, Timothy Julius Flock was the last of the trio to start his driving career. Before it was over he had outshone his siblings by becoming a two-time champion and the winner of 40 events in the major league of his sport.

Like many of his era, Flock learned his driving skills at an early age from the best—bootleggers from his family and acquaintances. He was usually the one to drive a decoy car to divert the attention of revenuers from the cars transporting the illicit whiskey. He learned well.

During NASCAR's formative 1948 season he was among the winners

Tim Flock

Two-time winner of the Winston Cup

as he took the first checkered flag in a modified car race at Greensboro, North Carolina, over the established stars of the day. When NASCAR introduced its new car "Strictly Stock" division in June 1949, Flock and his brothers were there. His oldest brother Bob—the hardest driving one of the trio—was the event's pole winner and the driver Tim started next to on the dusty three-quarter-mile track. The middle brother, flamboyant Fonty, started fifth in the 33-car field. When the day was done, Fonty emerged in second place, Tim was fifth and Bob had become the day's first casualty, after being the first driver to lead a lap in the division's history, after the engine failed on the pole-winning Hudson after just 38 laps had been run.

The new division's second race was held in early July on the beach and road course in Daytona where NASCAR had begun the prior season. In it the Flock family would make history. Not by winning—that honor went to fellow Alabamian Red Byron who finished just one place ahead of Tim. The family's distinction in that race lay in their numbers. In addition to the three brothers, the field also included three women, one of which was the Flock brothers' married sister, Ethel (Flock) Mobley. It marked the only time in the

first 50 years of NASCAR competition when four siblings competed against each other in any of the major events. (She finished 11th in her husband's Cadillac, ahead of both Bob and Fonty who were sidelined by engine maladies—she never let them forget it at future family gatherings either!)

Tim's early success was just an indication of what lay ahead. He would win 40 races and take pole honors 37 times on his way to two driving titles. In 1955, his best season, he won 18 races in 45 starts in the potent Chrysler 300s fielded by Carl Kiekhaefer. It was a record which stood a dozen years before being surpassed by Richard Petty's 27 in 1967. The 1955 season also saw the youngest Flock take 19 pole awards, a record which still stands as the sport celebrates its 50th anniversary.

Took 19 poles in 1955—a record which still stands as NASCAR hits its 50th year

Tim, the last of the racing brothers, despite illness, was present as NASCAR began its 50th anniversary celebrations at Daytona in 1998, but died shortly thereafter. He was the last of the famed family which has played such a part in NASCAR's rich history.

Any list of the greatest drivers in stock car racing history finds Fireball Roberts at or near the top. Even though he never won a championship, his prowess on the tracks, his skill behind the wheel and his daring style made him one who the fans came to watch. More often than not, he gave them their money's worth.

A native of Daytona, Edward Glenn Roberts Junior earned his nickname Fireball through his skill as a school baseball pitcher. Although replacing this time driving races in the Modified and Whelen

Fireball Roberts

divisions, Roberts was second in the inaugural Southern 500 at Darlington's new track and finished second to champion Bill Rexford in that season's points race. His early skills were displayed in 1958 when he won six times and garnered sixth in the points in just ten starts.

He topped qualifying 35 times during his career and posted top-five finishes in 93 of his 203 starts

With the advent of super speedways in the early 1960s, Roberts shone. He was the first pole and race winner when the new big track in Atlanta opened in 1960, and was the first to top qualifying the same year on the then new Charlotte Motor Speedway. The year before, he had won the inaugural July race at Daytona Speedway from the pole and led every lap in winning a 250-mile race on the 1.4-mile Marchbanks Speedway in Hanford, California. The latter feat marks the only time any driver led every lap of a major race on any of the circuit's track of a mile or longer. He was the first to win the pole, a qualifying race and Daytona 500 during Winter Speedweeks on his home-town track, a feat he accomplished in 1962.

Roberts' solid frame and rugged features gave him the image of a professional athlete. It was a persona he took seriously and carried well. Always accessible to the news media, Roberts willingly bore the mantle as a spokesman for his sport.

His 33 career wins encompassed the full spectrum of challenges racing offered. He triumphed on big tracks and small, dirt and paved, road courses and ovals. He topped qualifying 35 times during his career and posted top-five finishes in 93 of his 203 starts. He was a leader in nearly half the races he ran.

Roberts was fatally burned in a wreck in the opening laps of the 1964 World 600 at Charlotte. His passing left a void. Those who had watched him drive knew they had seen the best at work.

As a short but wiry child, Everett Owens had a shock of hair that looked like the cotton raised in the Piedmont area of South Carolina where he lived. Folks around there started calling him "Cotton Top", but just the first part of the nickname stuck as he grew up.

When word later spread to the dirt tracks of the area that "Cotton is running", the race drivers at that track knew who they had to beat. Now hidden under a driver's helmet was the light-colored topping of the top Modified driver, Cotton Owens. He won more than 100 feature events in the 1950s, before shifting his time and talent to the bigger arena of Winston

Cotton Owens

Drove Pontiac to first major league win

Cup (née Grand National) racing. There, too, he was successful as he went six straight years with at least one victory.

Cotton Owens, in a Pontiac which clocked in at 143.198mph, was the fastest qualifier for the 1959 inaugural Daytona 500, a race which saw him finish fourth. Two years earlier, when racing was still on the beach-road course along the city's junction with the Atlantic Ocean, Owens had won the big race and given Pontiac their first victory in NASCAR's major league.

While he loved driving, Owens felt his talent lay in working on the cars and making them perform. He became a car owner and picked a local Spartanburg youngster named David Pearson as his driver. They teamed for 25 victories and the 1966 championship.

Early in their association, Pearson was having trouble getting to victory lane. Owens dropped his wrenches, donned his helmet for a final time and drove a second car in the fall race at Richmond, Virginia. Owens beat Pearson and the rest of the field and showed his pupil how to win. It was the fifth and final victory for the veteran cotton-headed driver who now shares his skill and knowledge with his three racing grandsons on the dirt tracks around his Spartanburg home in South Carolina. It is an area not too many miles west of the Darlington oval where Owens had been the top qualifier and pole winner 40 years earlier.

Won more than 400 Modified and Late Model Sportsman races before becoming a successful car owner in the 1960s

With himself and other drivers in his cars, they won 39 Winston Cup events from 1950 until Owens retired in 1973. They also won 37 pole positions. Included in the victory list was a triumph in the 1960 inaugural Atlanta 500 with Miami's Bobby Johns behind the steering wheel. Owens' other drivers included Buddy Baker, Bobby Isaac, Junior Johnson, Ralph Earnhardt, Marvin Panch, Bobby Allison and Fireball Roberts. All of them, as well as Owens himself, were voted to the list of NASCAR's greatest drivers.

Care-free, curly-headed Joe Weatherly was a winner before he ever climbed into a stock car. His early success had come astride the snarling Harley-Davidson motorcycle which carried him to a trio of championships. But he moved from two to four wheels with aplomb and found added success.

The first sight of future auto greatness for Joe Herbert Weatherly came in the 1953 season when he won the NASCAR Modified division crown racing on the tracks around his native Norfolk, Virginia area. Wild and fun loving both on and off the track, "Little Joe" was a big man behind the wheel of a race car.

His first victory in the major

Joe

The Clown Prince of Racing

Weatherly

Little Joe rides tall in a driver's seat

league of stock car racing came at Nashville, Tennessee in 1958. It was the beginning of a 25-victory career cut short at Riverside, California's road course a half dozen seasons later.

Very superstitious, Weatherly was adverse to the color green. He once drove sockless in a race because his blue socks faded to green when he walked through a puddle prior to a race. He simply removed the offending footwear and put his trademark saddle oxford shoes back on his bare feet. He also shunned a pay-off in green dollars after winning at Darlington. Bob Colvin, the Darlington Raceway president, made good on the pay-off with a wheelbarrow full of silver dollars. Weatherly also once slept in his car rather than take the room given him by a hotel. The room number was "13". Such antics, plus riding a donkey in the Southern 500 pre-race parade, earned the ever-smiling driver the title "Clown Prince of Racing".

Winner of the Grand National championship first in 1962 and again in 1963, despite running in only the major events

Weatherly's career also included a dozen victories in NASCAR's Convertible Division which ran in the late 1950s. Among those were several which resulted in stirring duels with friend and cohort Curtis Turner when both were driving the topless Fords for the Pete DePaolo stable, which later became Holman-Moody. But his major success came in the Grand National cars where he won the 1962 championship driving for the car owner Bud Moore. Moore opted to run just the major events and Weatherly still won the title for the second straight year. He was chasing a third consecutive crown when he was fatally injured at the California road course in the first major event of the 1964 campaign.

A hard competitor and loveable clown who seemed to speak in a rapid, staccato shorthand, Weatherly enjoyed life and excelled in every form of racing he tried. He left the sport a champion.

A man for all ages in NASCAR is Oregon's Herschel McGriff. He drove in the 1950 inaugural Southern 500 and still competes four decades later.

A lumberman by trade, his skills behind the wheel have seen him racing in the Mexican Road race, at Darlington's oval, on the road course at Riverside, California and on the short tracks in the country's southeast. He won many of them, but was admired by the vast majority of the drivers he defeated over those seasons.

For a dozen straight seasons (1981–1992) his fellow competitors in NASCAR's Winston West division voted McGriff the Most Popular Driver. The span included the 1986 campaign when he also won the Winston West Championship.

The 1954 season, prior to a 17-year hiatus when he returned to his

Herschel McGriff

Won NASCAR races in last six decades

lumber business, was his best on the east coast. That year he accepted the offer to drive Frank Christian's Oldsmobiles. Even though he took Christian's offer after the season began, he would take four victories in his 24 starts and post 17 top-ten finishes to rank sixth in the year's final point standings. It was a strong finish for the handsome driver. In the year's final six events he scored four wins including the season finale in the race at North Wilkesboro, North Carolina. He was second only to Lee Petty in the next to last race of the campaign the prior week at the Martinsville, Virginia oval.

Ever youthful, McGriff continues to enjoy his sport and avocation well into the 1990s as he nears his 70s. He frequently races in Winston West and Featherlite Southwest Tour events to escape business pressures. He also follows the NASCAR Craftsman Truck Division to see how his son-in-law Chuck Brown (married to McGriff's daughter Debbie) carries on the family's racing heritage in the organization's newest circuit.

A pioneer of racing's rough and tumble beginnings and a skilled competitor over much of the history, McGriff was always a tough customer to race against whether the battle was on a rutted dirt track or the smooth pavement of a super speedway. Yet when the cars pulled back into the pits after the battle, McGriff was a friend to all his foes and an inspiration and adviser to the younger drivers.

For a dozen straight seasons he was voted most popular driver in Winston West division

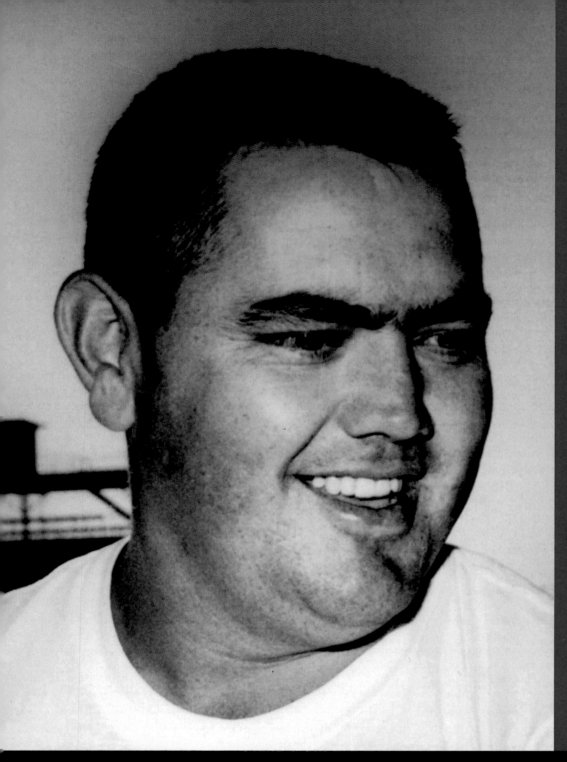

The heavy set youngster was not sure why he was being called behind the mule as they ploughed the field, but he responded to his older brother's yell. He was delighted when he found out the purpose of the work's interruption. His brother wanted him to race a car at the local North Wilkesboro track in the blue hills of North Carolina. He would run in the fill-in event between the races. It was a "Moonshiner's race"— named after the cars used in the illicit trade of the era.

Junior Johnson

50-time winner in a 15-year career

Robert Glenn Johnson, Junior, didn't win that day as he would often do in the future. But the contest began the storied career of the driver known at various times as the "Wilkesboro Wild Man", the "Ronda Road Runner" and most often as Junior Johnson.

His career spanned just 14 years and one of those was spent as a "guest of the government" after he was caught building a fire under his father's whiskey still in the mountains near his home. He readily admits he delivered the family product and quickly points out it was the only way to make a living during those times in Appalachia. The "business trips" did teach him how to handle a car on a twisting road and how to avoid capture—those would-be abilities which he translated to race tracks later.

Winner of the Winston Cup six times as team owner—including three consecutives

He won his first major race in June 1955 on the third-mile track at Hickory, North Carolina. His 50th and final victory came on his home track in North Wilkesboro in the fall of 1965. Between those two came triumphs at Daytona, Charlotte, Atlanta, Darlington and all of the other major facilities of that time. He was the first driver to win two events at Charlotte's mile-and-a-half speedway when he won the fall races of 1962 and 1963. The second led to his early retirement at the age of 35.

As dramatic as his power slides on dirt tracks and fearless as his style on pavement, Johnson hung up his helmet after the final race of the 1965 season. He then started a career as a team owner fielding cars that won 119 races and took the Winston Cup championship six times—including three consecutive in 1976, 1977 and 1978 with Cale Yarborough as his driver and three more during the 1981–1986 span when Darrell Waltrip occupied the seat in Johnson's cars. Johnson-owned machines also won the pole position 129 times and led 582 of the 838 races they started.

Retiring from the sport completely in 1995, Johnson can still smile when he recalls the day that he had to put his shoes on to drive his brother's car. It beat looking at the back of a mule.

Luck played a role in Ned Jarrett's move from working at a North Carolina sawmill to racing on the nation's NASCAR tracks. His skill at cards won him an automobile in the summer of 1953. He now had the chance to race. He made his first start at the local Hickory oval in late August. Labor Day, the first Monday of September, found him in the car at Darlington. He lasted just eight laps before an oil line failed. Not the best start for a future Hall of Fame driver.

Ned Jarrett

Winner of the Winston Cup in 1961 and 1965

CAR #11

He raced on the big time circuit infrequently over the next five years, preferring to hone his skills on the short tracks of the Sportsman division of NASCAR. He learned quickly and he used his present to bet on the future. By 1957 he was the division's champion, a title he earned again the following season. (The Sportsman division later became the current Busch Grand National Division.)

Jarrett's success was enough to make him move up to the division of competition now known as Winston Cup. Picking his events, he won twice during the 1959 campaign and five more times the following season. Although he won just once in 1961, he was able to be consistent enough to get 23 top-five finishes and another 11 top tens to earn his first coveted championship success.

He took the honor and accepted the responsibility of the title. His early years had left him shy, and having to work at an early age to help support his family left him uncertain when speaking in public, an obligation he felt he had to fulfil as the best of his sport. He took the Dale Carnegie public speaking course to overcome his deficits, not knowing the speaking talents he learned there would lead to an entire new career after his racing stopped.

Before he retired at the end of the 1966 season he would amass 50 career victories and the 1965 championship. Included among the 50 was a win at Atlanta and the most lopsided victory in Southern 500 history, a 14-lap margin over second-place Buck Baker in the 1965 edition of the Labor Day classic. He also won a short track event that year by twenty-two laps over the closest challenger.

After he retired from driving, he was an award-winning promoter at the Hickory track and went on to a career as a highly respected television announcer on CBS and ESPN races.

Came out on top of the most lopsided victory in Southern 500 history—by 14 laps

It was in his role as color commentator that he was able to call his son Dale's first career victory at Michigan Speedway in 1991 and the memorable description of his triumph in the 1993 Daytona 500. He felt lucky to do both… But luck has been playing a part in his whole racing life.

Rex White

1960 winner of the Winston Cup

As time neared for the start of the 1961 campaign, White needed to renew his state driver's license. That required the parking ability. It was a circumstance seldom called for on the dirt or paved tracks where he plied his trade.

After several unsuccessful attempts he finally did get his street car correctly positioned and had the slip to prove it. He was nearly as proud of the renewed permit as he was of the Championship trophy.

At the time, a valid state license was required for a NASCAR driver. It is a condition since dropped, but worrying for White at that time.

His Championship had not come easily. The season was nine races old before he won. But when the year's 44th and final checkered flag had flown, White was there. In his 40 starts he finished out of the top ten positions only five times. Such consistency, along with his half dozen victories, earned him the crown as the best in his sport in 1960.

The 1961 season was nearly as good as his title campaign as he added seven more wins and wound up second to Ned Jarrett in the season's championship hunt.

In his 40 career starts he only finished out of the top ten on five occasions

Piloting a white and gold Chevrolet with a bold, red number "4" emblazoned on the door, White would go on to eight more victories and a dozen more top qualifier awards during his nine-year career. He was ranked in the top ten of the standings in six of his nine seasons of full-time racing.

When he retired following the 1966 campaign, he had started 233 major races and led one out of every five. Nearly half of the races he ran saw him finish in the top five.

Not too bad a career for someone who had trouble parking.

Blond and handsome, the former carpenter from Elmhurst, Illinois first tried his hand in **NASCAR** competition in 1957. He ran seven events with little success. Discouraged, he returned to the midwest and resumed his efforts in United States Auto Club (USAC) events. There he achieved the success he sought. He won their stock car crown twice.

Bolstered by that success, he again headed south in 1960 back to the NASCAR ranks. Success came, but not quickly. He was in the second season of

Fred Lorenzen

Winner of 26 Winston races

his return before he broke the ice with his first victory. It came at the half-mile oval at Martinsville, Virginia. He went on to win two more events that season. The next opened many eyes along the pit road. It came at the treacherous Darlington egg-shaped oval where he not only won, but did so after topping the qualifying runs. His third victory came at the mile-and-a-half Atlanta oval. The northern upstart was beating the sport's established stars and doing it on their home turf.

He was signed by Ford to drive for the Holeman-Moody operation out of Charlotte, North Carolina. He quickly became their top star and the wins continued at a pace that earned him the nickname "Ford's Golden Boy". He won at Daytona, Charlotte and Atlanta. He was the first driver to win three straight races at Bristol and did the same at Martinsville. During the 61-race 1964 season he ran a limited schedule making just 16 starts. But he won eight of them and wound up 13th in the year's point standings even though he did not start 46 of the races.

Always a fidgety, nervous sort, Lorenzen was troubled by ulcers late in his career. His 26th and final victory came in a 100-mile qualifying race prior to the 1967 Daytona 500 and he finished second to Mario Andretti in the big event.

In the 1963 season he won six of his 29 starts and took the pole nine times. His success was sufficient to make him the first stock car driver in the sport's history to win more than $100,000 in a single season as he topped the year's earning chart at a whopping $122,588. (35 years later a driver can win that much in a single race.)

Lorenzen was the first driver in NASCAR history to win more than $100,000 in a season

He retired after the 1972 campaign and went on to become highly successful in real estate around the Chicago area. When he left racing, he did so with a record of 26 wins in his 158 starts. Over half of those races saw him leading the field and finish the race no worse than tenth.

Lorenzen came a long way from his first venture into NASCAR's ranks. During his initial stab he once had to chip away at a junk yard windshield to make it fit his race car. In the mid 1950s, "Fearless Freddy" Lorenzen couldn't afford to buy a replacement. When he left the sport, he definitely could.

Marvin Panch

Winner of the 1961 Daytona 500

adopted home track near his Daytona residence, Panch was asked to drive a sleek gull-wing Maserati in a major sports car event. He didn't particularly like the car but wanted to wring it out so some sports car driver didn't outrun him. With a full 36-gallon gas tank, he was putting the car through its paces on Valentine's Day when the front end lifted as it flew into the track's 31-degree banked third turn. Unable to steer, Panch felt the car drifting toward the retaining wall, hit, flip onto its roof and slide down the track. It stopped on the grass apron as fire erupted. Panch was trapped inside as the car rested on the doors which comprised the roof. He feared he would burn to death.

He might have but for five men, stock car drivers and mechanics, who were returning from lunch when they saw the wreck. Big Tiny Lund was one of them. They hurdled the fence and tipped the flaming car enough to open the door and pull Panch to safety.

Badly burned, Panch asked his stock car owner Glen Wood at the hospital to allow Lund to drive in his place at the Daytona 500. Wood agreed. (Lund and the four men were all awarded the Carnegie Heroism Award for their actions.) Lund went on to win the race in the red and white Ford, never changing a tire in the 500 miles and running out of gas on the final lap.

Although told he may never drive again, Panch did not accept the prognosis. Before the season was over, he not only raced anew but won two poles and took a win at North Wilkesboro. He would go on to sweep the two races at Atlanta in 1965 and won the World 600 at Charlotte in 1966.

He retired after the 1966 campaign but left a record of 21 poles earned in his 216 starts. He won 21 times—about once in every ten starts—and had a record of 96 top-five and 126 top-ten finishes. Much of his success came after being told his career might be over.

Winner of 17 career NASCAR Winston Cup races—including eight from 1963–65 for the Wood brothers

They called him "Tiny" for the same reason some people call a bald-headed man "Curly". At six foot five inches and 250 pounds, the Iowa native was anything but small—neither in talent nor stature as a race driver.

He won just five races in NASCAR's major league, but one of those was the 1963 Daytona 500, a victory which would make most drivers' careers.

His peers and those who followed the sport of stock car racing voted DeWayne Lund into the list of the Top 50 drivers of NASCAR's first half century not only for that quintet of triumphs, but also for the hundreds of other races he won in the Sportsman division races (now known as Busch Grand National) and for his three championships in the NASCAR Grand American division, which battled on

Tiny Lund

Winner of the 1963 Daytona 500

the short tracks, as well as his title earned in the Grand National East competition that ran both short and big tracks in the mid-1970s.

Fun loving and a master of dirt track competition, Lund moved from his native state in the mid-1950s in search of more competition. He found it in South Carolina and the surrounding states. There he could race four of five times a week and exhibit the skills honed on the dirt of the country's heartland. He became a frequent winner even against the top names in NASCAR.

His big break came on Valentine's Day 1963. Returning from lunch with friends, he saw a car crash as they entered the track. Knowing someone was in trouble, the big man drove to the spot, jumped the fence and helped pull the driver from the flaming wreckage. The driver was Marvin Panch, slated to drive the potent Wood brothers Ford in the following week's Daytona 500. A grateful Panch asked the owner to let the man who had saved him take his place in the car. The Wood brothers agreed and Lund drove to the first and biggest win of his career.

Lund went on to win five more Winston Cup races and was a six-time pole winner. A hard but heady driver, his 303 starts in the big league resulted in him finishing in the top ten 119 times—better than one out of every three races.

Usually punctual, Lund was late for the pre-race driver's meeting at Talladega in August 1975. He'd qualified A.J. King's dark blue Dodge 31st in the 50-car field and had high hopes for the race. He apologized to NASCAR officials for his tardiness and went to his car to make his first start in over two years. In the seventh lap, as the field exited the 33-degree banking of the second turn and headed down the 4,300 foot long backstretch, a multi-car wreck occurred. Lund's car sat crumpled when the dust cleared. It had been "T-boned" on the driver's side by another car. Lund was killed by the impact.

He finished in the top ten 119 times out of 303 starts—better than one out of every three races

Ironically, the race was won by Buddy Baker, a big man too and a long-time fishing buddy of Lund's. The two had spent many a day fishing and joking with each other at Lund's Cross, South Carolina fishing camp. Baker and racing both lost a big friend that day.

Like many drivers in the late 1950s, Bobby Isaac grew up poor and not well educated. He did know, however, how to drive a car. It was an ability he discovered at an early age and a talent he honed, like many drivers of the era, on the rough-and-tumble dirt tracks which dotted the Piedmont around his Catawba, North Carolina home.

His wiry build and tenacious style made him a driver to beat on the dusty ovals. His lack of schooling, however, made him shy. Even when he won at the tracks like South Carolina's Greenville-Pickens or Columbia Speedways or

Bobby Isaac

Won 37 times out of 308 starts

Concord, Hickory or Asheville in his home state, he was most apt to hide in the infield with friends than be embarrassed when he could not sign an autograph.

His skill in a race car was recognized. By the early 1960s, he was asked to drive cars in NASCAR's major league. By 1964 he was mounted in a factory-backed, hemi-engine equipped Dodge at Daytona. In his 100-mile qualifying race, prior to the 500, he came to the wire for a three-abreast photo finish. The camera showed Isaac's car first to the line. He had won in the big league of stock car competition and on its biggest track.

1970 Winston Cup winner with a career tally of 47 races, 13 poles, 11 wins and 32 top-ten finishes

He was married now, to a former school teacher. She had taught him to read and write. It was a skill he needed that February day as he was besieged by fans asking for autographs. A broad smile swept across the crew-cut topped face. He gladly complied.

The thrill of winning on the highest level was a pleasant change. It brought him recognition and more offers to drive top cars. One he accepted came from Nord Krauskopf and Harry Hyde, owner and crew chief for the K&K Insurance Dodge team. it was a combination which worked.

During the 1969 season, they won three races and as many poles. It was just the beginning. The following year they teamed for 17 victories and took a record 20 pole position awards and led 35 of the 50 races they started.

To some, the 1970 season might have been a let down, but not for Isaac and his team. They were on the pole 13 times in the 47 races and won 11 with 32 top-ten finishes. Their consistent performance throughout the campaign saw them emerge as the champions of 1970. The 1970 season also saw the team, with Isaac driving, set a speed record of 201.104mph in a NASCAR-sanctioned run at the huge Talladega Speedway.

Isaac retired from Winston Cup racing in 1976. He had posted a record of 37 wins in his 308 starts – a victory in every eighth race – and 50 pole positions with 170 top-ten race finishes.

He returned to his racing roots and succumbed to a heart attack at Hickory Speedway in August 1977. He was buried at the cemetery adjoining the track where his skill as a race driver first emerged.

Bobby Isaac's success

Growing up in Spartanburg, South Carolina, David Pearson was exposed to racing at an early age. The area was a hotbed for fast cars. He quit his job at a local textile mill and put what money he had or could borrow into a beat-up race car. As uncertain as the move seemed, it was the start of one of stock car racing's best careers.

His natural talent quickly drew attention as he outperformed better cars and older drivers. By 1960, he had moved up to NASCAR's big-time circuit where, as a rookie, he put his car in the top five in three races with four other top-ten finishes, and won a pole. The sanctioning body named the driver

David Pearson

Little David the Giant Killer

haired youth the division's Rookie of the Year. It was just the beginning.

In 1961 car owner and master mechanic Ray Fox tapped the Palmetto State youth to drive his Pontiac in the major races. They scored their first win together in Charlotte's World 600 and went on to win two more super speedway races. David Gene Pearson was soon known as "Little David the Giant Killer" in press accounts. No one previously had won three of the big track races in one season.

Cotton Owens, himself a great former driver, picked Pearson to drive his cars in a quest for the championship. Their best season together came in 1966 when they won 14 times, took eight poles and were crowned the championship team.

Midway through the 1967 campaign Owens and Pearson parted as Pearson became the driver for Ford's Holman-Moody operation. It would be even more successful. In the blue and gold number "17", Pearson won the 1968 and 1969 titles, 26 poles and 32 races.

Even more success lay ahead. In 1972, the Wood brothers were searching for a driver. A.J. Foyt had returned to the USAC races and Donnie Allison, Foyt's successor, had gotten ill. They asked Pearson to try their car. In just 14 races that year they won six.

The 1973 campaign may have been the best. Although they ran a limited schedule of races they won 11 of the 18 they started that season, and were the year's top money, race and pole winners. During Pearson's stint with the Woods (1972–79) they won 43 races and took pole honors at Charlotte Motor Speedway an unprecedented 11 straight times. They also won the 1976 Daytona 500 in a last-lap wreck with Richard Petty and won the Winston 500 at Talladega three straight years. Pearson won ten times on the venerable Darlington track and topped time trials on an yet-to-be-beaten 13 occasions at the track dubbed "Too Tough to Tame".

Pearson, by now known as the "Silver Fox" for his sly style

Three-time Winston Cup champion—second on all-time list with 105 victories and 113 poles

which never showed his potential until he needed to, had a record of 105 victories, 113 poles and three championships when he retired after the 1986 season. His poles and victories have him ranked second in both categories as NASCAR celebrated its 50th anniversary more than a decade later.

Not too bad for a man who gambled his savings on a race car to escape toiling in a textile mill.

In the summer of 1958, a 21-year-old youngster from Level Cross, North Carolina first placed his distinctive signature on a NASCAR entry blank when he got his cousin to help him tow a 6-year-old convertible to the half-mile dirt track at Columbia, South Carolina for a race. It was the youth's father's car and he wanted to test himself. It was just ten days since he had come to the age which allowed him to get a NASCAR license.

The kids were a little concerned when they qualified. This is supposedly an unbreakable sport. But they warily persevered. He drove well enough to finish sixth in

Richard Petty

The man they call
the King of NASCAR

battling some of the sports biggest stars like Fireball Roberts, Bob Welborn (the defending Convertible Division champion), Glen Wood and Larry Frank. He avoided the frequent accidents, stayed out of the leaders way as they passed him five times during the 200 laps and brought the car home in one piece.

Such was the beginning in one of the most famous careers in stock car racing history. It was the birth of Richard Petty's 200-victory, seven-championship career and it doesn't even show in his records of Winston Cup competition. It was a race for another division.

Petty's unique, scrolled and flourishing signature first appeared on a major league entry blank for a race later that month at the one-third mile Canadian National Exposition Speedway in Toronto. It was a 100-lap race for which he qualified seventh in his dad's second car to which they added a "1" in front of Lee Petty's more familiar "42". (He would not get his famed "43" until the following season.) The second generation driver acquitted himself well in his first big-time venture. He watched his mirror and moved out of the way when

Won 27 out of 49 races in 1967— including a record string of ten in a row

leader Cotton Owens came up behind him. Owens got around the cautious driver, but the second place challenger didn't. He hit the back bumper of the youngster's car sending him into the fence and out of the race. The offending car went on to win. Lee Petty, the disappointed youngster's father, was the driver.

Despite the setback, Richard Petty would go on to Rookie of the Year honors in

1959. He scored his first victory the following year on the half-mile dirt track at the Charlotte (NC) Fairgrounds two weeks after finishing third in the Daytona 500. The latter was a race he would win an unprecedented seven times before retiring as "The King" of his sport after the 1992 season.

Petty's best and most dominant season came in 1967. That year he won 27 of the 49 races including a record string of ten in a row, and finishing second in seven others to cruise to the second of his seven crowns. His win in the 1967 spring race at Darlington was the 55th of his career, one more than the record for a career set by the man who bumped him out of his first race nearly a decade earlier— his father, Lee.

Petty's colorful autograph appeared on a record 1,184 entry blanks and on tens and thousands of items offered by fans. He was, win or lose, the last driver to leave after most races. He stayed to sign every program, slip of scrap paper or ticket stub. It wasn't a quick scrawl, but a signing which would look more at home on the Declaration of Independence.

He learned it when taking, at his father's insistence, a course at a local business college after high school. His handwriting was atrocious. The course required a penmanship class with the practice of scrolls, loops and clarity. From that came the signature of the most successful driver in stock car racing, Richard Lee Petty.

Won Daytona 500 an unprecedented seven times in a 200-victory, seven-championship career

LeeRoy Yarbrough

A 14-win career

Yarbrough grabs his first major win in the 1969 Daytona 500.

Panch, the Pettys, and the other stars of stock car racing. He was also smart enough to know he needed more experience. He returned to short track sportsman racing in 1961, but was back on the major circuit in 1962.

He caught even more eyes when he won the 300-mile Modified-Sportsman race held at Daytona the day prior to the 500. Before the season ended, Yarbrough was occupying the seat of a factory-backed Pontiac fielded by Indiana's Ray Nichels. It was where he wanted to be, in a solid car and racing against the best in the business.

Won the Daytona 500, World 600 and Southern 500 in 1969—before the days of the $1 million bonus

On a dusty half-mile oval in Savannah, Georgia, where he had run and won many times in the under divisions, Yarbrough scored his breakthrough victory as he lapped the field in a year-old Plymouth owned by Louie Weatherby. It was the first career win for both owner and driver and one of two they'd score together during the 1964 campaign. Among the drivers he defeated on the rough Georgia oval was another young driver named Cale Yarborough. Their presence together would cause a lot of confusion among fans and announcers as their careers progressed and their successes became more frequent. Although their last names were spelled differently—just one "O" in LeeRoy's family name, two in Cale's—the similarity drove those watching or calling the events to use first names as they often battled each other for victories.

The LeeRoy versus Cale calls became frequent during the 1968 season as the two won eight times in their Fords. LeeRoy won two as driver of the potent Junior Johnson entry and Cale won six at the controls of the Wood brothers' mount. Although they often fought each other for the lead as in the inaugural NASCAR event at Michigan in 1969, they finished one-two just four times.

That 1969 campaign was Yarbrough's best. In 30 starts he finished in the top five half of the time and won seven. Among the victories were wins in the Daytona 500, World 600 and Southern 500, the richest, longest and oldest big track races of the circuit. A decade and a half later such a performance would have won the high-school drop-out The Winston $1 million bonus awarded any driver to win three of the big four races. (The Winston 500 at Talladega, added to the bonus later, was bypassed by many of the top teams, including Yarbrough's, in 1969.)

Yarbrough also tried his hand at the Indianapolis 500, a race which fitted his daring driving style. But he was severely burned in a practice wreck and became hooked on the pain relievers he had to take. His career spiralled down hill and he died in a Florida mental hospital in 1984, a dozen years after he drove his final race.

Yarborough was a driver of Junior Johnson's number 98.

He grew up poor, without electricity in his grandmother's home in rural Wilkes County, North Carolina. From the rustic home they could see the end of the power line and he could hear the roar of race cars from nearby North Wilkesboro Speedway.

He had lived with her while his parents went to Detroit in search of work. It was a hard life but one which built character and instilled determination in the young Benny Parsons.

After high school he moved back to his parents' home and he joined his father as a mechanic at a taxi car company. There he learned about cars as he repaired and tuned them. He even filled in on busy days as a driver. It was an introduction that meshed well with

Benny Parsons

The nice guy of NASCAR

the temperament and untried talents of the husky youth.

Some friends were going to a race at an area track. They asked Parsons to join them. He agreed and was enthralled with what he saw. Before long he was driving in those local events, whetting the skills that would lead him to the pinnacle of stock car racing.

As the 1960s progressed Parsons became a regular on the Midwest Auto Racing Circuit (MARC) which would become the Automobile Racing Club of America (ARCA). He won and became the organization's 1968 and 1969 champion. The latter year found him winning their biggest race, the 300-mile event during Daytona's winter speed festival. He had some help from Ford's racing division and they offered to continue the assistance if he wanted to move up to NASCAR's major circuit. He jumped at the opportunity.

He won his first NASCAR race in 1971, his second full season in stock car racing's major league. It came in a 100-mile event at Virginia's South Boston Speedway.

By the time he retired from driving in 1988, he had posted 21 victories and won the 1973 Winston Cup championship. Among his victories was one over Darrell Waltrip in the 1980 World 600 at Charlotte and a triumph in the 1975 Daytona 500. Also included on his NASCAR résumé were 20 pole positions. One of those, at Talladega in 1982, saw him become the sanctioning body's first driver to exceed the 200-mile-an-hour barrier as he hit a speed of 200.176.

His victory list included some lasts, also. Parsons was the winner of the final race at Texas World Speedway at College Station and he won the final two NASCAR events at southern California's Ontario Motor Speedway. Parsons' 21st and final triumph came in the 1984 spring 500-mile race at Atlanta.

Retiring in 1988 he could look back on a 21-win career—including the 1973 Winston Cup championship

After hanging up his helmet, Parsons, one of the nice guys in the sport who always remembered names and faces, went on to an award-winning career of explaining his sport to television viewers and radio listeners. His expert commentary on ESPN earned him an Emmy from the television industry in 1996.

Parsons' Winston Cup championship trophy and the Emmy share the spotlight in his home. He also has electricity, the luxury he lived without while growing up.

A.J. Foyt

Four-time winner of the Indy 500

Whenever a list of the great American race drivers, without designation of the type of racing, is assembled, one name is certain to appear— A.J. Foyt.

The Houston native won in sports cars at Sebring, Le Mans, Nassau and Daytona, in Indy Cars including four Indy 500s, in sprints and midgets. And he won in both USAC and NASCAR stock cars. He is, arguably, the best race driver ever. He even won a 1964 match race in horse-drawn sulkies against Parnelli Jones on the mile dirt oval at the Indiana Fairgrounds.

Foyt was already a luminary in motorsports when he made his first run under the NASCAR banner in 1963, a year he led three races and had two top five finishes in five starts. He won his first race at the sanctioning body's home track in Daytona with his triumph in the July 1964 Firecracker 400 in a Ray Nichels Dodge. The following July he was again the honoree in the event's post race celebration in victory lane, this time driving a Ford.

In 1972 Foyt's talent and skill earned him a motorsports distinction shared by only one other driver. That year he won the Daytona 500 to join Mario Andretti as the only race drivers in history to win both the Indianapolis 500 and Daytona 500 in their careers. It is a feat no other driver who tried both has achieved. Not Bobby or Al Unser. Not Cale Yarborough or Roger Ward. Not Bobby or Donnie Allison, or Parnelli Jones.

Foyt never ran more than seven NASCAR events in any season. But he made the most of the seven he tried during the 1971 campaign. He won four poles and was victorious in two races with two additional top three finishes. Starting one race less the next season he also enjoyed two trips to victory lane, was on the pole three times and had four of his six races result in top four finishing positions.

Over 29 years of competition he raced 127 times under the NASCAR banner, with seven wins and one out of four starts resulting in a top ten finish. He led in 53, nearly all of those races against the best stock car drivers on earth.

Only two drivers in motorsport history have won both the Indy 500 and the Daytona 500. A.J. Foyt is one of them

His 128th and final NASCAR start came in the 1994 inaugural Brickyard 400 at his Indianapolis Motor Speedway. It was a race he had campaigned to have occur. It wasn't a race he won or even led. But "Super Tex" was beaming broadly when he was among the drivers running at the finish, and proud to have been part of the history made when NASCAR cars raced for the first time on the track where so much motorsports history had been made.

But A. J. Foyt had been making racing history throughout his long and fabulous career.

The years he spent as a building constructor made the heat and rigors of racing events in NASCAR's big-time Series incidental to Harry Gant. Roofing buildings, digging footings and hanging drywall were work. Racing was his pleasure and one he did well.

Gant's home town of Taylorsville, North Carolina, was the site of many a small oval-track battle, and it was there in the 1960s that the Tar Heel native first tried his hand at stock car racing. Initially racing in the Hobby class for two years, Gant soon quickly moved through several divisions until he was running — and winning — regularly in the Sportsman Division — later known as the Late

Harry Gant

18 wins and 208 top-ten finishes

competition which became the Busch Grand National Series in 1982, a division which had Gant as winner 21 times.

Between 1973 and 1978 Gant stuck his racing toe into the bigger pond of Winston Cup racing. He tried his hand at a few races – never more than five – while still competing regularly in the Busch events. The break came when he was tapped in 1981 to help Hollywood world land speed record holder Stan Barrett, the original driver of the Skoal Bandit cars owned by Burt Reynolds and Hal Needham. Gant's superior talent and racing experience soon placed him in the green and white machine as the primary driver.

Gant gave the movie folks their first victory as he drove their car to a win in the spring race at the tight Martinsville track in Virginia. Late that season, in October in Charlotte, he got the first big track win. Gant and the Skoal team were on their way. They won at least once every season for the next four years.

Gant's "Handsome Harry" title was replaced by "Mr September" in the 1991 campaign when he tied the modern-era record of four straight wins with consecutive-week victories at Darlington, Richmond, Dover and Martinsville. He even sweetened the string by also winning the preliminary Busch races the day before the Richmond and Dover Winston Cup events. The 1991 season was Gant's beat with five wins, a pole and 17 top tens. He also led the most laps—1,684—during the year and finished a career-high fourth in the final points ranking.

Gant's final career win came at the two-mile Michigan track in 1992 when, at age 51, he beat Darrell Waltrip and Bill Elliott in the August heat.

In the 1991 campaign he tied the modern-era record with four straight wins

After each of the victories, Monday mornings found him back at a work site near home, building or remodelling another structure.

At age 53 Gant retired from Winston Cup racing after completing the 1994 season. His 474 starts had afforded a record of 18 wins, 17 poles and 208 top-ten finishes. It also saw him at the head of the field in 192 of those races.

He walked away from the sport's major league, but could look back with pleasure on the career he built by doing something he enjoyed. But Harry Gant had been building something most of his life.

Too young to drive under NASCAR rules, William Caleb "Cale" Yarborough crawled under the garage fence to get to his race car at the 1957 Southern 500 at Darlington Raceway. The stocky, athletic youth, who had boxed in Golden Glove and been an all-state high school full back, wanted to be in the 500-mile classic so near to his Timmonsville home.

He was caught, twice, by NASCAR officials. Each time they threw him out of the pits, he got back in. He drove the race, too, only to have a hub fail and sideline his dream.

That tenacity and determination

Cale Yarborough

Three-time winner of the Winston Cup

stood him in good stead as he continued to chase his dream of becoming a race driver. He even accepted a job sweeping floors at the Ford-backed Holman-Moody shops in Charlotte to be close to the sport in case an opportunity came along.

Cale, still yearning for a chance to show his talent, picked up rides from time to time, usually in also-ran cars, just to be noticed. He got a car for the 300-mile Modified-Sportsman preliminary to the

Too young to drive under NASCAR rules he crawled under the garage fence to get his first ride

Daytona 500 in 1962 and promptly finished second. In mid-season of the 1963 campaign he took over driving for Herman "The Turtle" Bean, a graduate chemist from Tennessee who had driven with a tortoise-and-the-hare philosophy. Bean drove like the former. Yarborough emulated the latter. Bean almost fired the brash blond for wearing out tires!

The break for Yarborough came n 1965 when he was approached by Ken Myler, a former Petty Enterprises mechanic-turned-car-owner. Together they got their first victory, at Valdosta, Georgia in June. A dozen more top-five finishes that season landed the plucky driver in the seat of Banjo Matthews' factory Ford for 1966. He promptly finished second in the Daytona 500 and repeated it in the next race, another 500 miler at Rockingham. By the end of the season, he'd begun a five-year association with the famed Wood brothers team, where he would win 13 times and take pole honors on 19 occasions. Among the victory list were three straight Atlanta 500

The only driver in NASCAR history to lead a 500-lap event from start to finish

triumphs, a consecutive trio of victories at Daytona and wins in the initial two June races at the new Michigan Speedway.

In the early 1970s, he tried his hand at Indianapolis, but was soon back in the NASCAR ranks where he teamed up with legendary car owner Junior Johnson. It was the start of a great marriage. Johnson wanted his cars to run in front, as he had driven them. It was a style that fitted Yarborough perfectly.

They won immediately and often. Yarborough gave Johnson what he wanted in their first win. It came at the short Bristol oval in the spring race where Yarborough started from the pole and led all 500 laps of the race. It was the only 500-lap event in NASCAR history that was won without a lead change. Together through the 1980 season they won 55 races and took the Winston Cup championship an unprecedented three straight years (1976, 1977 and 1978).

Yarborough and Johnson parted ways after the 1980 season, but both continued winning. In 1984 Yarborough became the first driver to qualify for the Daytona 500 at more than 200 miles an hour.

By the time Yarborough retired at the end of the 1988 season, he had amassed 83 victories, including four in the Daytona 500 and a record five in Darlington's Southern 500. He also won 70 poles and ranked second in his sport's all-time list of lap leaders.

Now a team owner and voted into multiple Halls of Fame, Cale Yarborough no longer has to sneak under the fence to get in race tracks.

Growing up in South Florida, Robert Arthur Allison was too small for the usual high school sports. But he was drawn to the car races at nearby Hialeah Speedway. He watched and thrilled to the battles among Ralph Moody, Banjo Matthews, Red Farmer and the other local stars.

Soon he was able to borrow a car and another name (he was underage and didn't have his parents' permission). Shortly "Bob Sunderland" was a contender in the weekly races. A photo of a trophy presentation caught "Pop" Allison's attention. He told his oldest son that if he was going to race, to at least use his real name. Bobby complied and the career began. He continued racing the Modified events with the

Bobby Allison

Founder member of the "Alabama Gang"

victories coming more frequently. In 1961 he even tried his hand in NASCAR's major division. Yellowed record books show him finishing 31st in the 1961 Daytona 500's 58-car field. It did not forbode the future.

Small in stature but big in heart, Allison was a three-time winner of the illustrious Daytona 500 (in 1978, '82 and '88)

Always a quick learner, Allison realized he needed more experience. He returned to the open wheeled Modified-Special division where he won the championships in 1962 and '63 and won the title in NASCAR's oldest division – Modified – the next two years. During the period he had also followed Red Farmer to the Hueytown community near Birmingham, Alabama. He was soon joined there by his younger brother, Donnie. When the local drivers saw the trio pulling into their track you could almost hear them exclaim, "Oh Oh, Here comes that 'Alabama Gang'." Thus a title was born.

By the 1966 season he was ready to return to the sanctioning body's big league. He ran well in his maroon and white Chevelle but hadn't won by mid-season, an oddity for the tenacious Allison. To make things worse, he blew up his last engine during the Northern Tour event at Bridgehampton's road course on Long Island. On the way to the next race at Oxford, Maine, he stopped by a Chevy dealership where he found a replacement engine block. He called the Oxford track where they arranged a working space, after hours, at their local General Motors dealer. Allison, his brother Eddie and a friend (your author) worked to rebuild the motor well into the following morning. With little rest Allison took the Chevelle and its replacement engine onto the one-third mile track and won the pole. He went on to win the race, too, before the largest sports crowd in Maine history. He won twice more before the season ended. He was on his way.

He drove for and won with some of the biggest teams in the sport. He earned victories in Chevrolets, Fords, Mercurys, Buicks, Matadors, Dodges and Plymouths. He won on big tracks, road courses and short bull rings. Never a shrinking violet, he banged fenders with Petty, Pearson, Waltrip and Yarborough.

Allison's best season came in 1972 when he drove the Coke Machine Chevrolets for Junior Johnson. In their 31 starts they won 11 poles and ten races with a dozen more second place finishes. They also led in each of the year's first 30 races.

He suffered career-ending injuries in a first-lap accident in 1988 at Pocono. It was the year he won his third Daytona 500 this time with his son, Davey, finishing second. It was his 84th and final victory in a career of 718 starts over 25 years. His aggressive nature didn't prevent his peers from voting him the sport's most popular driver six times, and the media named Allison Driver of the Year three times.

He drove for some of the biggest names in the sport. He won on big tracks, road courses and short bull rings. He banged fenders with the best of them

Too small for regular sports, Allison showed racing measures heart, not stature, when figuring greatness.

The progression seemed natural for the athletic youngster in Owensboro, Kentucky. Having found success in go-kart races in his home area, he thought it time to move up to the late model stock car races which ran weekly at the local track. Assembling a car from junk yard pieces, he painted it with available colors. The result was an ugly brindle brown, but to young Darrell Waltrip it was a beauty.

His natural skill moved him quickly to the top of the heap in local battles. He looked for new worlds to conquer and found one at the paved oval at the

Darrell Waltrip

Winston Cup winner in 1981, '82 and '85

Tennessee Fairgrounds in Nashville.

As the 1960s ended and a new decade began he had already won the track championship at his new home. He was the driver to beat every week. He again sought new dragons in need of slaying. A new super speedway had opened in Alabama, at Talladega. It was the biggest and fastest facility in motorsports. It was there the brash but articulate Waltrip chose to make his big time debut. Borrowing money from his father-in-law he got a Mercury and headed for Alabama. He qualified mid-way in the 50-car field and ran well until the engine, untried at the sustained 190-mile-an-hour pace, came apart a third of the way through the race. In July he went to Atlanta and recorded his first top ten finish. Encouraged he returned to Talladega for the summer race and was not among the leaders, although he was one of them until his engine again failed in the event's second half. He found the thrill and challenge he sought.

His breakthrough victory came at his old home track, Nashville, in 1975 when he beat the best of NASCAR's Winston Cup division. It would be the first of 84 victories in his long career.

He was soon offered rides by other teams. DiGard was the first and he gave them 26 victories between 1975 and 1980. As 1981 neared Cale Yarborough announced he was leaving Junior Johnson. The seat was open and Johnson tapped Waltrip to fill it. It was the start of a relationship which would dominate the sport for the next several seasons. In their first two campaigns together they won a dozen races each year, earned 18 pole positions and swept the Winston Cup championships both years. The victories kept coming. They won six in 1983, seven the next year and in 1985 they won the inaugural running of the Winners-Only "The Winston" all-star race at Charlotte. They also won the following

His breakthrough came at Nashville in 1975—the first of 84 victories in a long and distinguished career

Waltrip battles young Davey Allison, on the high banks.

day's World 600 race. It was the third of a record five times Waltrip would win the longest event in stock car racing. The Waltrip–Johnson combo went on to win their third championship that season.

Even after he left Johnson to accept a ride with the Rick Hendrick team in 1987, the wins kept coming. Among them was a victory in the prestigious Daytona 500. It finally came in 1989, in his 17th try. In 1992, the second season after he started his own team, he also took another long-sought prize as he won the Labor Day Southern 500 at Darlington, the oldest 500-mile event in NASCAR and the tough track where he had won four spring races.

From his start as a brash, outspoken youth, Waltrip mellowed to become an elder statesman and popular spokesman for his sport. He also served as an expert commentator for television coverage of races, a field he may accept as the next challenge. His wit and insights make him a natural. Just as his skill and ability took him to the top on the track.

Teaming up with Junior Johnson in 1981 was a major success. The pair went on to the Winston Cup three times

It was only natural for the strapping youth to follow his famous father's tire tracks into stock car racing. Born in South Carolina but raised one state north, the Charlotte resident grew up to the roar of racing engines and the smell of hot rubber. Much of his childhood was consumed at the dirt tracks which dotted the south-east quadrant of the country. Summer vacations were spent working on his dad's race car and changing tires during pit stops.

Buddy Baker

242 races, 19 wins and 40 poles

With a given name like Elzie Wylie Baker, Junior, it wasn't difficult to understand why he gravitated toward being called "Buddy". His dad, the two-time NASCAR champion, was always referred to as Buck.

As soon as he could after high school, Buddy Baker was in a race car. Learning the tricks of the trade, the variables of the tracks and the messages sent the driver through the suspension of the car. He had to learn to run on the edge of disaster without going over—when to charge and when to lay back. The first he learned well. The latter, many think, is something he never quite grasped.

Driving his father's cars he honed his skills starting in 1959 on the dirt track in Columbia, South Carolina. As he progressed, the offer of better cars came his way. Finally, in 1967 he was offered the seat of the factory-backed Dodge owned by master mechanic Ray Fox. They jelled as a team with Baker getting his first career win that fall in the 500-

He loved the big tracks— Buddy was the first driver in NASCAR history to run a lap in excess of 200 miles an hour

mile race at his home town track, Charlotte Motor Speedway. The following season they won again, also at the Charlotte facility in May's 600-mile grind. The 1968 campaign also saw them win four poles.

Baker loved to go fast. The big tracks—Dayton, Talladega, Charlotte and Atlanta—were his cup of tea. In a test for Chrysler at Talladega early in 1970, Baker became the first driver in history to run a lap in excess of 200 miles an hour. He was clocked at 200.447 on the 2.66 mile, high-

banked track. It was on that track, in the mid-1970s, that Baker became the first—and so far only—driver to win three straight races.

Nor were his skills limited to fast tracks. At Darlington, the tricky, oldest big oval where speeds are 25 miles an hour lower than places like Daytona or Talladega, Baker also won back-to-back races. His 1970 triumph in the Southern 500 was particularly satisfying to the husky second-generation speed merchant for it came in the race and on the track where his father had won three times during his stellar career.

At Talladega, in the mid-1970s, Baker became the first—and so far only—driver to win three straight races

His victory in the 1980 Daytona 500 marked the first time any 500-mile auto race had been run in less than three hours. His winning average still stands as the event's record as the sport celebrated its 50th anniversary nearly two decades later.

Baker retired from competition after the 1992 season with 19 wins, 40 poles and was a leader in 242 of his races. Baker, one of five drivers who join their fathers on this top 50 list, remains active in the sport. His knowledge is employed by teams who ask him to test for them. He also relates his insights, often humorously, as an expert commentator on CBS and TNN racing telecasts.

Buddy Baker was not only successful in following his father's tire tracks. He left some pretty deep ruts of his own.

Flamboyant and unconventional were words used to describe the dashing and handsome Tim Richmond when he first migrated from the ranks of Indy Car racing — where he was the Indy 500 Rookie of the Year in 1980—to NASCAR's premier circuit. But they also had to add words like talented, fearless and skilled to the list of descriptive adjectives.

In his first year on the NASCAR scene, as he learned the new tracks and heavier machines, he didn't even produce a top ten finish. But driving second-pack cars he was soon able to challenge the top teams as he proved to be a "quick study" in the new discipline.

Tim Richmond

Winner of the 1993 Daytona 500

In 1982, just his second full season in stock car racing, he proved to be a winner. His breakthrough triumph came on the serpentine layout of Riverside Raceway in southern California when he defeated a stellar field. (The next four finishers in that race are all in this list of the top 50 drivers of NASCAR's first half century.) Richmond proved the victory was not a "fluke" when he repeated it at season's finale that fall on the same track.

Moving from the J. D. Stacy team to Raymond Beadles' Blue Max operation in 1983 Richmond won again. The win came at Pocono's three turn oval in the mountains of Pennsylvania where he not only won but did it after winning the pole. The challenging track proved to become one of the Ohio bachelor's best. He won there four times.

Perhaps Richmond's best run came in 1986 when he joined the Rick Hendrick team and worked with veteran crew chief Harry Hyde. From late May through early September, a 12-race stretch of the season, they scored an

astounding six wins and posted four more second places. He finished the 1986 campaign with seven victories and eight pole positions, both tops for the season for NASCAR's biggest circuit. They finished the year third in the points chase, just six behind second place and three-time champion Darrell Waltrip.

The following season, although gravely ill, Richmond ran just eight times in 1987. Even with the limited schedule he was able to post a pair of victories, win a pole and finished among the top ten in half of those races.

Came to the NASCAR Winston Cup series after an IndyCar career and won 13 races

The relationship between Hendrick, a young and highly successful Southern businessman, Hyde, the crusty but wise veteran crew chief, and Richmond, a flashy and colorful midwesterner, was turned into the plot for the movie *Days of Thunder*.

Richmond's place on the NASCAR scene lasted just seven years. However, his 13 victories and 14 poles testified to the skill and ability he displayed during the short stay. He passed away in 1989 but left an indelible mark on his chosen field of endeavor.

The many NASCAR champions have all taken numerous routes to reach the pinnacle of their sport. Some followed a family lineage. Others went racing when other sports paled. For some it was progression of testing themselves more critically as they moved up the ladder of motorsports success.

Growing up in hot south Texas, Terry Labonte spent his early youth racing quarter midgets. It was a family affair. His dad, Bob, an air-frame engineer, would prepare the small open-wheeled cars and his mother would fix the food and look after toddler Bobby, the driver's younger brother. Terry was a

Terry Labonte

Two-time winner of the Winston Cup

Consistency took Labonte to two Cup championships

heady and smooth young driver who won often in the open-cockpit racers.

    As he grew older, Bobby took his place in the midgets and Terry moved on to the short track stock cars that raced around their Corpus Christi home. He was good at that, too. So good that at the end of one season he had to chose which point lead he would try to defend, the one on the dirt tracks or at the asphalt ovals. He opted for paved and won the title driving his dad's cars.

    During that time the Labontes met and raced against a Louisiana businessman, car owner and sometime driver named Billy Hagan. A few years later, Hagan had moved into NASCAR's Winston Cup ranks with a car that carried Skip Manning to the circuit's Rookie of the Year title. Hagan offered young Labonte a job with the team as a mechanic. It was the "foot-in-the-door" the young Texan had sought. Following a mid-season dispute between owner and driver, Manning left the team just before the 1978 Southern 500 at Darlington. Hagan tapped Terry to drive even though he had neither raced in NASCAR's major league nor been on a big track, much less one as tricky and treacherous as Darlington. Nor had he ever run so long a race—500 miles.

Finished in the top five in his first race on the big-time circuit— fourth in the 1978 Southern 500 at Darlington

"Texas Terry", "The Iceman", finished fourth in his first start.

Terry qualified the car a respectable 19th and was determined to finish the race. Pacing himself as the laps ticked away he battled heat and fatigue. He noted the scoreboard 100 laps, 200, 300, 350. He concentrated on the laps in the long, gruelling event. He never noticed the positions. Finally the lap count reached 367, 500 miles. He'd made it. He was curious about the congratulatory waves and comments as he returned to the garage. Asking Hagan why, the owner pointed to the scorebaord. Showing in fourth place was his car number. "Texas Terry" had finished in the top five in his first race and done so on one of the most demanding tracks.

Two years later at the same track, they won the Southern 500. It was the first victory for Labonte as a driver and the first for owner Hagan. But there would be more. Two triumphs and another seven top-finishes were theirs in 1984 as they won the Winston Cup championship.

A decline in the oil exploration industry cut sharply into Hagan's business and racing operation. In 1987, Labonte was driving for legendary car owner Junior Johnson. In their three years together they won four times and also took a victory in 1988's "The Winston", the sport's all-star, winners-only event.

Labonte joined Hendrick Motorsports in 1994 and his winning ways continued. He won three times that season and an equal number the next. In 1996 he won just twice, but put together a consistent year that saw him win the coveted Winston Cup title a second time.

With more than 20 victories and 26 poles, the youngster from the steamy southern tip of the Lone Star state has become known as "The Iceman" for his cool demeanor on the tracks and his calmness under pressure. His brother, Bobby, hasn't done too badly either, becoming NASCAR's champion in 2000.

Studious and quiet, Alan Kulwicki was different from the common concept of what a professional race driver should be. He came to NASCAR's major league in 1985 with an engineering degree and was the first driver to arrive at the garage carrying a briefcase.

A Wisconsin native and lifelong bachelor, Kulwicki had a plan for his career. He wanted to own, work on and drive his own cars. It was a concept which he had worked in the highly competitive American Speed Association competition in the midwest..

He sold all his ASA equipment and headed south, to North Carolina and NASCAR racing.

Alan
Winner of the 1992 Winston Cup
Kulwicki

He tried just five races in 1985 and ran 23 the next season, but only had one fourth-place finish to show for his efforts. Things improved in 1987. He finished second to Dale Earnhardt at Pocono, had two more top-five and six top-ten finishes and won three poles—but the breakthrough victory still hadn't come.

As the 1988 campaign wound down Kulwicki still hadn't found the key to the victory lane in the major league of stock car racing. That November he found the hiding place under a cactus at the mile oval in Phoenix, Arizona, as the Winston Cup Series made their inaugural run at the track. He had started his Ford 21st in the field and been a contender throughout the event. When Ricky Rudd's engine went away in the 296th lap of the 312 at stake, Kulwicki

He was the first driver to arrive at the garage carrying a briefcase

pushed his Ford to the fore and was never headed. He celebrated the victory and his ethnic heritage by spinning his car around at the start-finish line and taking a lap backward around the track in what he referred to as his "Polish Victory Lap." It was a popular win among his peers as they had watched him struggle to make the grade in the sport.

Four year later, now with five victories under his belt, the Cup competition came down to the season finale at Atlanta. Now Kulwicki was challenging for the title. A race long duel had Kulwicki's Ford and the Ford piloted by Bill Elliott battling for the win and the championship. Kulwicki used his skills at math and managed to lead one more lap than Elliott. The leader bonus points earned thereby gave him the narrowest point margin (10) in championship history.

He was making a personal appearance prior to the Bristol race the next spring. As he flew to the track the plane went down. Kulwicki was killed in the crash. His career lasted just seven seasons—but his performances were sufficient to have his peers place him among the sport's top 50.

Geoffrey Bodine

18-time race winner in Winston Cup

To achieve success in any of NASCAR's major divisions is a major challenge. But to do so in three of them is a feat known to few drivers. One of them, Geoffrey Bodine, has been a big winner in NASCAR's Modified, Busch Grand National and Winston Cup arenas.

The steps to follow seemed logical to Geoffrey Bodine, who had started racing micro-midgets when he was just six years old. He would try a bigger class and when he mastered it, try the next one.

He applied his plan to the diminutive cars at his family's track in New York, became a winner and moved up to the starter class of stock cars. He was soon winning those on a

regular basis. He advanced to the powerful NASCAR Modified division. He not only won there, he became the terror of the circuit, winning against the present, past and future champions of the division.

As a kid he heard NASCAR's big division—then called Grand National and now Winston Cup—was coming to race at nearby Watkins Glen road course. He caught a ride to the track with older friends and watched the "big cars" race from his perch in a tree along the backstretch. He thrilled at the sight and knew it was where his future had to take him.

Along the way, he found time to take engineering courses at the junior college near his home town in Chemung, New York. It wasn't that he wanted a career at a drafting table or in a manufacturing plant. He studied the curriculum so he could make his race car safer and faster. Applying what he learned, he finished second in the 1977 Modified points race.

An offer came to build and drive a car for Emanuel Zervakis on the Busch Grand National circuit. It meant moving south, to Richmond, but it also meant the next step in his plan. He accepted. Bodine was soon the scourge of the division as he had been in the open-wheeled Modified circuit. Living in a small trailer and working on the cars day and night, plus driving them on weekends, he was able to tolerate the pace. He won six times on the circuit. It was time for the next step—the Winston Cup.

He tested the waters for a couple of years. Three races in 1979, five in 1981, the year he introduced a workable power steering mechanism to NASCAR's major league. It was, indeed, where he felt he should be. He moved to North Carolina, near Randleman, where his hero Richard Petty resided. By 1982 he plunged headlong into NASCAR's biggest division. He won his first pole that season, at Daytona in July, but wouldn't crack a winner's circle until 1984 at Martinsville, a track where he had already won in Modified and Busch competition.

At the start of the 1984 season a young Charlotte car dealer named Rick Hendrick was starting a team. He picked Bodine as his driver after discussing the choices with Harry Hyde, the shrewd veteran master mechanic. Unsponsored, they won three pole and three events during the 1984 campaign. It was the beginning of the Hendrick Motorsports operation which won the final four Winston Cup titles in NASCAR's first 50 years.

Along the way, Bodine was joined in the sport by younger brothers Brett and Todd. All three were in the field for the 1994 inaugural running of the Brickyard 400 at Indianapolis Motor Speedway. The event was historic, not just because it marked NASCAR's first time at the venerable track, but also because all three of the family's siblings led. It was a first time three brothers had led any event in the track's long history.

By 1996, Bodine, with 17 victories to his credit including the 1986 Daytona 500, owned his own team. That year he added an 18th win to his credentials when he drove to victory at Watkins Glen. On his cool down lap after the victory he drove slowly down the backstretch, peering to the left. He was trying to find the tree where he'd watched the "big cars" of NASCAR race decades earlier.

Bill Elliott

When a race driver wins he has to beat all the others. It usually makes him pretty unpopular with the other's fans. But that has not been the case with Bill Elliott, a lanky red head from northern Georgia who has won a lot of races but also been voted the sport's most popular driver a record 15 times.

The hills of north Georgia had spawned its share of bootleggers and given rise to some of stock car racing's early pioneers. Drivers like Gober Sosebee and Sarah Christian. The former a top modified driver in the NASCAR ranks. The latter the best early female throttle stomper.

The red clay hills were also the source of another racing family. The father, George, had a junk yard where his three sons could tinker with old cars, get them running and race them through rusted hulks. The boys, Ernie, Bill and Dan, even converted a former class room at an abandoned school next door into a shop where they worked, stripping parts off one heap and cannibalizing another to make a runable machine.

Three brothers, Bill at the wheel, and Ernie and Dan at the wrenches, tried to take NASCAR by storm

When, in 1970, they tired of battling each other, they transferred their focus to organized competition as they moved to the sportsman events at area dirt tracks. Bill, the best pilot of the trio, became the full time driver with Ernie and Dan twisting the wrenches. They did the family proud as Bill won with regularity in the beat-and-bang events. By the mid-1970s the Elliotts were on top of the heap and looked for new worlds to challenge. They chose the rapidly growing NASCAR Winston Cup circuit and made their first venture in the spring 500-mile event at Rockingham's North Carolina Motor Speedway.

Somewhat awed in the presence of drivers like Richard Petty, David Pearson, Baker, Allison and Yarborough, the Elliotts were happy just to qualify for the event. Starting 34th in the 36-car field their hopes ended in a plume of smoke as the engine in their Ford expired after just 32 laps. They tried seven more races that season, but never had a top-ten finish. Success was elusive, but they kept pursuing it for several years and drew attention with strong runs. In the 1979 Labor Day race, the Southern 500 at the venerable Darlington track, Elliott finished second to David Pearson in what proved to be the veteran's penultimate win. Although it wasn't a victory, it was an omen of what lay ahead.

Bill Elliott's first win came far from home on a road course. The breakthrough fell in the year after Michigan businessman Harry Melling bought the team from George Elliott in 1982. With Coors beer sponsoring the car, Elliott drove to victory on the southern California road course at Riverside in the 1983 season finals.

More wins followed as he was the victory lane honoree three times in 1984 and voted the Most Popular Driver for the first time. He would enjoy his best year in 1985. Starting with a victory in the season-opening Daytona 500, Elliott went on a tear. He won a record 11 races and the "The Winston Million", a $1 million bonus for any driver who won three of the big four races of the year—Daytona 500, Winston 500, World 600 and Southern 500. Three years later he won just six races, but put together a season which saw him crowned Winston Cup's 1988 champion.

In 2000 the Chrysler Corporation announced its return to NASCAR racing with a team headed by Ray Evernham, who picked Elliott as lead driver. The veteran speed merchant began by winning pole for the season opening 2001 Daytona 500. Later in the season he also gave the new team its first victory at the Pennzoil Freedom 400 at the Homestead-Miami Speedway.

Through NASCAR's 53rd season, 2001, Elliott has accepted first place trophies at 41 races and has been voted the sport's Most Popular Driver an unprecedented 15 times, so many the award was renamed fro him that season. He also holds the absolute stock car time trial record of 212.809 mph set at Talladega in 1987.

Although a big winner, Elliott's shy manner and determination made racing's Huckleberry Finn a favorite even among other driver's fans.

"Awesome Bill" was the first to have a million dollar season.

Growing up in the Tidewater area of eastern Virginia, Ricky Rudd hung around his dad's auto salvage yard. It was natural his interests gravitated toward mechanics rather than the usual stick-and-ball sports. Tinkering with the old cars he learned how and why mechanical things worked. He was soon racing, with his family, in go-karts.

Winning championships as a teenager made it seem easy, so he moved on to the kidney-shaking sport of motocross where he was again a winner as he found that smoothness and consistency were more productive than recklessness and sheer speed.

Ricky Rudd

Learning about NASCAR the hard way

The area around his Chesapeake home was rife with stock car racing. It was the area which had spawned two-time NASCAR champion Joe Weatherly and journeyman driver Bill Champion. It was the latter who picked Rudd to drive his two-year-old Ford in 1975's spring 500-mile race at the North Carolina Motor Speedway at Rockingham. It was a big step for the 18 year-old, but one he wanted to take. With his family's permission he did.

In his initial venture in NASCAR's major league, young Rudd was able to qualify 26th in a 31-car field. With Champion's coaching and using his own head, Rudd came home 11th. It was the start of a career which entered the second half-century of NASCAR racing with the longest string of consecutive winning seasons among his peers. The next try came at the steeply banked Bristol half-mile where he pulled off a top-ten finish, but the freshman's luck ran out the following week at the mile-and-a-half Atlanta Raceway oval.

Ninth on all-time career-earnings list

Running well as the half-way mark of the 500-mile chase approached, the engine in his car let go as he came out of the fourth turn. Oil spilled under the rear wheels and the car spun backward into the inside wall which protected the pit road. Angry but unhurt, Rudd undid his belts and climbed from the machine ignoring the other cars whizzing past as they raced back to the caution flag he had caused. Champion was livid. Not at the engine failure, but because his youthful chauffeur had ignored the old racing rules of waiting until the field slows before undoing the safety equipment, and never leaving a disabled car from the traffic side. It was a lesson the high school honor student never forgot.

Rudd's big break came five years later. Now driving his family's owned and maintained Chevrolet, they went to the fall race at Charlotte. They stunned everyone by qualifying second (to Buddy Baker) as they out performed a strong field of factory supported teams. They went on to prove the time trial run omened their ability, finishing fourth in the 500-mile event. The display got him a ride with the DiGard team for 1981 where he won three pole positions. The following season he moved up to Richard Childress' operation. With Childress he scored his first career victory in the sport's major league. It came at Riverside's road course in June 1984.

Race winner for 17 consecutive seasons

It was just a start. Driving for owners Bud Moore, Kenny Bernstein and Rick Hendrick, before forming his own team in 1994, Rudd continued his winning ways with all of them. As NASCAR's first half century ended he had won at least one race every year for 17 consecutive seasons, a list extended in 1997 when he won the Brickyard 400 at Indianapolis and again that fall at Dover. It is a record second only to Richard Petty's 18-year run and the longest by any active driver. Not included in that string was a win at Dover in his first try at Busch Grand National competition and the 1992 championship in the International Race of Champions (IROC) series.

He has also blown engines and wrecked. But he never forgot the words of his old mentor, Bill Champion: stay in the car until the field slows and don't climb out the traffic side of a disabled race car. He also recalls the lessons he learned early on: smooth and consistent wins races.

Neil Bonnett had not planned on becoming part of the Alabama Gang with the Allison brothers and Red Farmer. The card-carrying union pipefitter was just looking for some diversions from his job when he started attending races at the Fairgrounds race track in his hometown. He admired the machines which raced and marveled at the skill of those who drove them.

When the pit area was opened to the fans after each night's races, Bonnett was among the ones entering. He studied the cars to see how and why they could do the things they did. He

Neil Bonnett

The fourth member of the "Alabama Gang"

asked questions of drivers and mechanics. Among those he came to visit with regularly was Bobby Allison. The veteran driver took a liking to the curious fan and invited him to visit his shop. The offer was accepted and soon Bonnett was spending his off time working on the race cars. They even let him build himself one to drive.

Gone was the grandstand seat. Under Allison's tutorage the young and affable Bonnett quickly became a race driver, although he kept up his union dues. When Allison got offers to race at two tracks on the same day, he accepted both and sent Bonnett to drive at the second track. Intended or not, Neil Bonnett became the fourth member of the Alabama Gang, banging fenders and swapping paint with Bobby, Donnie and Red. He started to win more frequently.

Back-to-back winner at Charlotte ('82 and '83)

By the mid-1970s he was ready to follow the gang into Winston Cup, the apex of stock car racing. He was offered a chance to drive the K&K Insurance Dodge by owner Nord Krauskopf and top crew chief Harry Hyde. They won their first season together—in 1977.

Two years later he was in the seat of the Wood brothers' Ford where he earned five victories including a win in the 1982 Charlotte 600-miler. It was a victory he would repeat the next season while driving for the Rahmoc team.

To Bonnett it made no difference how long or short a race. In addition to winning the 600 consecutively, he was also the first to win the season opening Busch Clash at Daytona, a 50-mile chase for the prior season's pole winners, for two straight years.

Not reflected in his 18 career wins and 37 pole positions was a triumph in the NASCAR-approved race in Australia early in 1988. He won the week before at Richmond and would win the next at Rockingham, but between those two Bonnett and other drivers crossed the Pacific and ran the first ever NASCAR-style race on the new down-under speedway.

Bonnett was returning from an amnesia-causing 1990 accident at Darlington and a two-year hiatus from the sport when he was fatally injured during pre-race practice for the 1997 Daytona 500.

Throughout his career he kept his union card in his wallet. He was at the top of their work-priority list for nearly 20 years—about the same duration he was at the top the field of his adopted sport.

When Davey Allison was old enough to know what he wanted, he chose to follow his famous father, Bobby, into the competitive world of motorsports. His father, the 1983 Winston Cup and four times Modified Series champion, gave him two pieces of advice. First, if you can't afford to go to a race, stay home. Secondly, if you break it, know how to fix it. The elder Allison knew his approach would make the son a better racer, and it did.

Davey Allison

1987 NASCAR Rookie of the Year

Developing a knowledge of the sport, Davey Allison started his career racing in the Late Model Stock ranks at tracks near the family home in Hueytown, Alabama. He was a fast learner and was soon a winner at the local tracks before moving on to the Automobile Racing Club of America (ARCA) ranks. Looking to the future, young Allison started testing his skills in the Winston Cup circuit in the mid-1980s—but it was in 1986 that he got his big break.

Old family friend Neil Bonnett had been hurt. A substitute was needed. Impressed with what Allison had done with lesser equipment, Johnson tagged him to fill in for Bonnett in the race at Talladega. The pressure was great.

He was finally in a good car and in the race closest to his home. He just had to do well.

He did. Qualifying seventh in a strong field, the youngster not only ran with the leaders, he led the race. Late in the race he had to take quick action to avoid a wreck. He got the Chevrolet completely sideways in the 33-degree banking of the second turn and saved it. He finished seventh, on the lead lap. His run so impressed veteran observers, he was offered a ride in the potent Harry Ranier-owned Ford for the 1987 season—the start of a highly successful pairing.

Running for Rookie of the Year honors in 1987 Allison promptly staked a claim on the title by qualifying on the front row for the season opening Daytona 500. Heads turned. He did not win at Daytona but he was victorious twice during the season, the first victory coming at the Alabama track. Later that season Allison won again at the tricky mile oval at Dover, Delaware. The second triumph made him the first Winston Cup rookie to win twice in his freshman season. He walked away with the season's rookie title. But it was just the beginning.

He led the most races on the circuit in 1991 and was the biggest lap leader the following season. He was the first driver to win the division's all-star race, The Winston, back-to-back and he racked up 19 career victories in just 191 starts. He also took pole honors at 14 races. Young Allison, now driving for Robert Yates who bought the team from Ranier in 1988, was a star.

He won at Richmond early in the 1993 season and had run well all year. He finished third in the division's inaugural race at New Hampshire in early July. Back home in Alabama the next day he decided to fly his newly-purchased helicopter over to the Talladega track where his old friend Bonnett was testing, he even asked Red Farmer to join him. When they got to the track tragedy struck. The craft crashed while landing in the infield. Farmer was hurt but Allison suffered fatal injuries. A great racing career died with him.

To be successful at NASCAR's highest level of competition you must have the skills to race well at its diversity of tracks—speedways, short tracks and road courses. As he concluded his 21st season in Winston Cup racing, Rusty Wallace's record shows he has had what it takes. The tally shows 23 big track victories, 24 on the short ovals and a half dozen road course triumphs.

Wallace came up watching his father win a trio of track titles around home in the St Louis area. It wasn't extraordinary for young Russell, "Rusty" they called him due to his

Rusty Wallace

1989 Winston Cup champion

sandy red head of hair, to want to race, too. Many sons want to follow their fathers.

Rusty started on the Missouri short tracks and was soon expanding his race horizons. He was 1979 USAC Rookie of the Year and the ASA champion by 1983. The next season, his first full year in NASCAR's Winston Cup Series, the young Missourian won that division Rookie title.

But he had tried his hand in NASCAR's big time before. Four years earlier he had started his first race. The ride was a Chevrolet owned by Roger Penske. The race was the 1980 spring 500 miler at the mile-and-a-half Atlanta Raceway oval. Wallace, though inexperienced on the big, high-speed tracks, qualified an amazing seventh in the new car to outgun such stars as Richard Petty, Darrell Waltrip and Bobby Allison. Using the skills he had learned on the bullrings of the midwest and with Penske's coaching he finished the entire 500 miles and would end up second to winner Dale Earnhardt. His feat was not unnoticed by the other drivers nor car owners.

The next few seasons saw Wallace running just occasionally in Winston Cup as he continued to hone his skills in ASA competition. In 1984, an offer to drive for veteran car owner Cliff Stewart brought him back south, back to NASCAR's big time circuit. He had a pair of top five finishes and two more in the top ten that year and another pair of top fives in 1985 along with four top tens. He was learning the idiosyncrasies of the tracks and other drivers. He learned well.

If at first you don't succeed, return to be champion

Joining forces with Raymond Beadle's Blue Max team in 1985 he was ready. They won the spring race at Bristol and were victorious again that fall at Martinsville. It was the first of a 13 straight years Wallace would be a victory lane honoree (through 1999's campaign). In 1987 he scored his first wins on road courses with victories at both Riverside and Watkins Glen. His big track triumphs started coming in 1988 when four of his six wins occurred on the super speedways—Michigan, Charlotte, Rockingham and Atlanta. He won six times in 1989 and put together other good runs to become the Winston Cup champion, edging Dale Earnhardt for the honor by a mere dozen points. That year he also won the sport's lucrative all-star, winners-only event, "The Winston" at Charlotte.

Although he learned to race on ovals, Wallace has six road course victories to his credit, the most by any driver, and is considered by many as the best road racer in NASCAR history, having won on all three such tracks where the series has raced during his career. Those represent a half dozen of his 49 wins. In 1991 he utilized his skills to take the International Race of Champions (IROC) title, as well.

The Wallace clan may have a racing gene in their make-up. Not only did young Rusty follow his father into the sport, now he can watch as his younger brothers, Mike and Kenny, follow the path. But Rusty doesn't have to look far to observe his siblings. A glance out the windshield or in the rear view mirror will suffice as the three Wallace brothers all battle in NASCAR's major league.

A 35-time pole winner, Rusty Wallace has led nearly half of his races and won nearly $25 million during a stellar career. Little did his father realize as his oldest son watched him race on the Missouri ovals, that the child would outdo the adult. But he couldn't be prouder. It's the way fathers are.

Dedication and commitment are apt words to describe Mark Martin. Those and tolerance for pain of both a mental and physical nature. He has all that and more, comprising the person who has become a major winner at several levels of stock car racing.

Standing in the driver's seat, he could barely see over the steering wheel as his father sat and worked the gas and brake pedals while little Mark steered the car on the back roads of their native Arkansas. Now one of the best in the major league of stock car racing, Mark Martin credits that for his skill in a race car.

Using the skills he learned when he could only direct, not control, the car, Martin has evolved into one of his chosen sport's best. However, it was not always that way.

Mark Martin

Two-time Winston Select 500 winner

While still a teen Martin quickly became the scourge of dirt tracks around Arkansas. He wasn't even shaving when he started winning races and earning track championships. He was soon moving to the nation's midwest where he evolved into one of the most successful drivers in the tougher American Speed Association (ASA) circuit.

In 1981, Martin came with a trio of ASA championships to try his hand at NASCAR. Running five races that year he won two poles but only had two top-ten finishes. He tried a full schedule in 1982 with just six top-tens in 30 tries, but was runner-up for Rookie of the Year honors. He tried again the following year, driving for four different owners with a third his best showing. He headed back to the midwest spending the next four years gaining experience, sharpening his skills and earning yet another ASA title.

Picked up by car owner Jack Roush in 1988 with four ASA titles to his credit, he returned to NASCAR with a vengeance. They had a second place and a pole that season as they built for the future. The 1989 campaign saw them finally win, at Rockingham in the fall, as they posted 15 top-five finishes and a third in the season's point chase. The wins came regularly after that. As the 1999 season ended, they had amassed 31 victories on NASCAR's toughest, most competitive circuit. Martin, in Roush's Fords, has finished second in the Winston Cup points battle three times. He was second by 26 points, in 1990, and again in 1994 (both times to Dale Earnhardt) and second to Jeff Gordon after the 1998 season. From 1989 through 1999 Martin has never finished lower than sixth in points. Martin wins elsewhere, too. On the Busch Grand National circuit Martin has won 37 times to become the winningest driver in the division's history and, in 1998, also won his fourth championship in the International Race of Champions (IROC) series.

Since the Busch Series was formed as a major division in 1982, a Busch-Winston Cup double header has been swept by one driver 13 times. The last four by Martin. He also won the Bud Shoot-out at Daytona (for pole winners only) that opened the 1999 campaign.

Since the start of the Winston Cup's modern era (1972 when the schedule was reduced to approximately 30 races a year) just six drivers have won four straight races. Martin is one of them. Perhaps his most stunning win came in the caution-free spring 1998 race at Talladega where he averaged a NASCAR record 188.354 miles an hour for the 500 miles.

Martin competed through pain. He anguished when his father, stepmother and a sibling were lost in a plane crash. He suffered physically from injuries in a wreck during final practice for Daytona's July race in 1999, but started every race thereafter despite a broken wrist, damaged ribs, a broken leg and needed back surgery he delayed until the end of the season.

For someone who learned to drive standing in his father's lap on Arkansas dirt roads, Martin now controls his racing fortunes by utilizing the well-learned traits which brought him to the top of his chosen field.

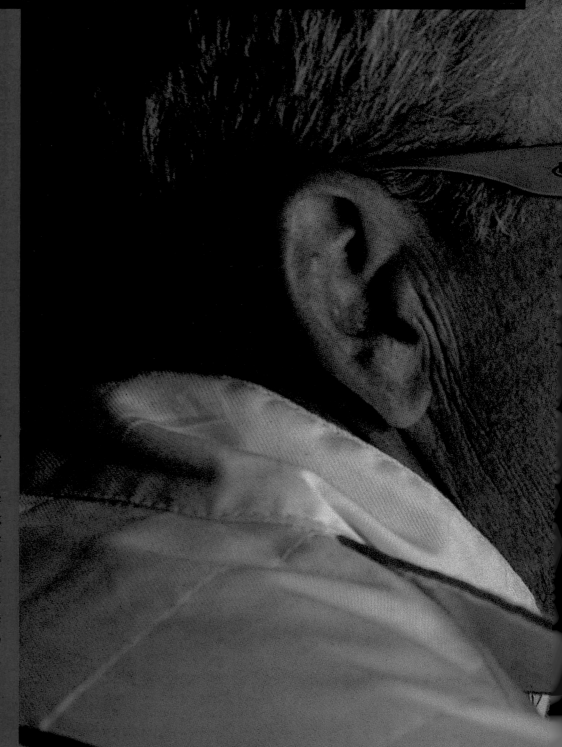

Dale Jarrett

1999 winner of the Winston Cup

"It couldn't happen to a nicer guy or to a better team," was the consensus along the pit road and in the NASCAR garage when Dale Jarrett and the Robert Yates team, headed by crew chief Todd Parrott, were crowned the 1999 Winston Cup champions.

They raced hard, clean and consistently throughout a gruelling 34-race schedule to earn the honor.

You also had to wonder if there was something genetic about reaching the pinnacle of the most competitive circuit in motorsports. Jarrett's success makes his family the second to see a second generation claim the title in NASCAR'S major league. They join the Petty family, Lee and son Richard, to have parent and child as champions.

Ned Jarrett was the circuit's 1961 and 1965 top driver.

Dale Jarrett is, in fact, one of five drivers on the list of the 50 best drivers of NASCAR's first half-century who is there along with his father. The Jarrett family is there with the Pettys, Bakers, Allisons and Earnhardts. A fifth of the list has a father and son sharing inclusion, too many for chance.

The second generation driver's racing career began on the paved one-third mile oval at Hickory, North Carolina near the family's home in Newton. It was a track he knew well from the years his famed father had been general manager and promoter there after retiring from driving in 1966 with the two Winston Cup championships and 50 career wins. The younger Jarrett, a skilled golfer and stellar four sport high school athlete, moved quickly up through the classes—Hobby, Limited Sportsman and Sportsman. He was successful, too, at other area tracks in the Carolinas and southern Virginia. By the mid-1980s, Jarrett had graduated to the Busch series where he became a first-time race and pole winner in 1986. He would win in the division, which ranks just below Winston Cup, 11 times and be top qualifier 14 times while running a limited schedule and starting to dabble in the major league. It was a division known as Late Model Sportsman prior to 1982 and which had Ned Jarrett as its 1957 and 1958 champion.

Dale dipped his throttle foot into the deeper pond a few times before going full time during the 1987 campaign. The next year found him tapped by retired Cale Yarborough to fill the seat in his car for the 1988 season, one which found him learning a lot from the three-time champion and 83 race winner.

As the 1990 season got underway he was driving for another of the great names in stock car racing, the Wood brothers of Stuart, Virginia. Another learning year in 1990 and a breakthrough season in 1991 followed. The team's four-year victory drought ended with

Jarrett's initial big league victory as he beat another second generation driver, Davey Allison, by a mere ten inches in the summer 400-mile race at Michigan's two-mile oval.

Now a winner in the most competitive division of motorsports, Jarrett was next sought out as the first driver for a new team being built by Joe Gibbs, the superbowl winning coach. They jelled quickly as they shared strong character and a demanding work ethic. With eight top-ten finishes in the team's building season, they were ready for 1993 to commence at Daytona. There Jarrett gave the coach his first NASCAR win. With his father Ned calling the action for CBS' live coverage, the younger Jarrett out duelled Dale Earnhardt for the victory. They won again in 1994 with a victory in the fall 500 miler at Charlotte. Jarrett was lured away from Gibbs after the 1994 season by team owner Robert Yates. In Yates' Ford and supported by a good team, Jarrett continued winning. They triumphed at Pocono their first year together and won four more times in 1996, including Jarrett's second Daytona 500 win and a victory in the Brickyard 400 at Indianapolis. The best was yet to come.

The 1997 season was great for Dale Jarrett. In the 32 races he won seven times, earned two poles, had 20 top fives, completed 99.5 per cent of his possible laps and led the most laps of any driver during the season. His efforts made him second only to champion Jeff Gordon in the points chase with the fourth closest margin in division history, 24 points. He was third in the 1998 points after wins at Talladega, Dover, Richmond and 19 top-five finishes which resulted in over $4 million in winnings for the season. The 51st anniversary season of Winston Cup competition (1999) found Jarrett earning a second Brickyard 400 victory among his four trophies and a season-high 29 top-ten runs on his road to the title.

The desire to win is a family trait for the Jarretts. But the sport has changed between generations. Dale's 1999 victory in the Brickyard 400 paid $712,240. In Ned's 13-year, 50-win, two-championship career he won $289,148. The 1961 and 1965 crowns were worth a total of $15,000 when Ned won them. The 1999 crown carried a reward of $5 million for Dale, but to Ned the pride he feels for his son's accomplishments is priceless.

Jarrett became a second generation NASCAR champion in 1999.

Growing up in the northern California town of Salinas, Ernie and his dad worked together to build his first race car in 1974 and they raced it on the short tracks which dot the San Francisco area of the state.

In 1977 they won the track championship at Stockton Speedway. It whetted the boy's appetite for more. He knew the southeast was the hotbed of stock car racing, especially the Charlotte area in North Carolina. It is where he headed. When he arrived he found it was not easy to get a foot in the door. Owners didn't want to let some West Coast unknown drive their car. But, Irvan was determined. Utilizing the welding skills he learned

Ernie Irvan

Winner of the 1991 Daytona 500

building his race car, he took a job welding together grandstands at Charlotte Motor Speedway while searching for a path into racing.

He finally landed a ride at the local Concord Speedway, just a few miles from his work site. He quickly became a regular winner. By 1987, he was a able to muster a car to drive in a few Winston Cup races. He took inferior cars and was able to race with the leaders, getting more from the machine than it should give. His all-out style and daring ability caught the attention of other owners.

By 1990, he hooked up with the Morgan-McClure team from Abbington, Virginia near the Bristol Speedway. It was on the team's home track that Irvan won his first pole in the year's spring race and they got the first victory in the fall's 500-lap race on the steeply banked half-mile. They won more, too, six times over the next three seasons including a victory in the Daytona 500, before Irvan was tapped by owner Robert Yates to succeed Davey Allison after a helicopter accident had claimed Allison in July 1993.

By the summer of 1994 the Yates-Irvan combo had won five times and were second in the season's standings, only 27 points out of the lead as the tour made their second visit of the season to Michigan's two-mile oval. In practice Irvan's Ford swerved suddenly and crashed, nose first, into the second turn's concrete wall. Irvan was hurt, badly. Doctors at the hospital where he'd been airlifted gave him only a ten percent chance of survival. But they were not aware of the pluck and determination in the damaged body. Although he missed the year's final 11 races, he led so many laps in the events he'd run, he won the year's award for leading the most laps during the season.

Months of recuperation and painful therapy followed. He was back in a race car just 14 months after the near fatal wreck. Despite the long layoff and a patch over his left eye, Irvan picked up where he had left off. He was competitive in the final three races of the 1995 season and was back to his winning ways with two victories in 1996.

The sweetest win came in 1997. When the circuit returned to the Michigan track in June of that year, Irvan was ready. Tentative in qualifying, he put the Ford 20th in the 43-car field. Dispelling any apprehension when the starting flag flew, Irvan quickly charged through the field and was back at the head of the pack. He went on to win the race and eke out a measure of revenge on the track which had nearly ended his career and claimed his life.

It was, however, again at Michigan in the summer of 1999, that the track wrought its revenge. Practicing for a Busch Series race, Irvan's car spun into the wall. The impact resulted in another concussion. This one, though not as severe as the crash five years earlier, made Irvan realize it was time to leave the sport he loved. It was more important to be there for his wife and family.

Yes, Irvan was a driver with pluck and determination; traits he coupled with great skill to be one of the best in his chosen sport.

A nation mourned when news filtered through that the greatest driver in the history of NASCAR had not survived a final-lap accident at the season-opening 2001 Daytona 500. A 76-race winner, Dale Earnhardt had metamorphosed from a hard charging youth with a slam-bang style to the elder statesman of his sport, albeit with the same style that had earned him the nickname, "the Intimidator." Still a winner—twice in 2000—he had visibly mellowed off the track.

Dale Earnhardt

Seven-time Winston Cup champion

He took pleasure watching his son, Dale Jr, win the Busch Series title in 1999 and 2000. He watched with delight as his son successfully chased the Rookie title in 2000, a distinction he earned 21 years before. He could pause and conjure his own path to racing stardom.

Some of his earliest childhood memories were from dirt tracks near to his home in Kannapolis, North Carolina, a small textile mill community a few miles north of Charlotte. Thinking back his mind saw the swirling red dust and his father Ralph's car banging fenders

The first driver to back up a Rookie of the Year title with a Series' crown

with the competition. He could again smell the hot oil and hear the roar of engines and the crowds in the wooden grandstands. He stirred anew to the shaking of his pick-up truck vantage point.

A restless youngster, Dale Earnhardt abandoned school in the eighth grade. He wanted to get a job in the local textile mill and make some real money. The hot, dirty work soon lost its appeal. The pay was not as much as he had thought. He sought a way out. He had to look no further than home and he quickly saw why his father loved racing cars. The freedom to do what your heart tells you to do. Still in his late teens, it was the path he'd follow.

He, too, was soon racing on the area tracks, albeit in the starting classes of stock car racing. He was so proud of his first car, built with advise—but not help—from his father. Preparing to go for his first race, he mixed left over paints from partially used cans in the shop and sprayed the car. It was bright pink! Undaunted, he raced and he was good from the beginning of his career. Soon he was winning.

His first try at the big time of NASCAR competition came from journeyman driver-owner Ed Negre. It was an offer to drive his Dodge in the 1975 World 600 at Charlotte Motor Speedway. He took the offer knowing the car was not a top ride. He took it because the car bore the number "8"—the number used so long by his father who had died, at his shop, of a heart attack two years earlier. He didn't come close to winning that day, ending up 22nd and 45 laps in arrears of winner Richard Petty. He was running at the finish and one place ahead of another young competitor named Richard Childress. They would be close again in the future.

Young Earnhardt ran a very limited schedule in the sport's big league over the next few years, but went full bore in 1979 when he won a seat with the new Rod Osterlund team. Going for Rookie of the Year honors they won four poles and won the spring race at the high-banked Bristol half-mile track. The team and driver went on to win the Rookie

title. The next season they won five times, including a first big track win at Atlanta, and took the Winston Cup championship. Earnhardt became the first driver in the sport's history to back up a Rookie title by winning the next year's Series' crown. The 1981 campaign saw Osterlund sell his operation and Earnhardt drive the final 11 events for Richard Childress, who had become a car owner.

Earnhardt spent the 1982 and 1983 seasons driving for veteran Bud Moore and winning three more times, before reuniting with Childress in 1984. Since they got together, the duo won six championships, a record 11 Daytona 500 qualifying racesas well as becoming the first to win "The Winston" all-star race three times. Earnhardt had also taken three IROC titles, including 1999, and won 21 Busch Series races, including the 300 at Daytona a record seven times. He had won on all types of track except a road course, but he added that to his laurels with a win at the twisting Sear Point track in 1995.

Arguably the best driver in NASCAR history, Earnhardt continued to pursue an eighth Winston Cup crown to break the tie with Richard Petty. He was close in 2000, winning two races—including the Winston 500—on his way to the runners'-up spot behind Bobby Labonte. Then came that fateful day at Daytona.

The 2001 season concluded Jeff Gordon's ninth full year in stock car racing's major league. But that time has seen the former midget and sprint car driver compile a record that that can be envied by racers with twice the longevity—58 victories including Daytona 500s, Brickyard 400s, five straight Southern 500s and Charlotte's 600 and 500, 40 poles, four championships plus over $45 million in winnings.

Jeff Gordon

Four-time winner of Winston Cup

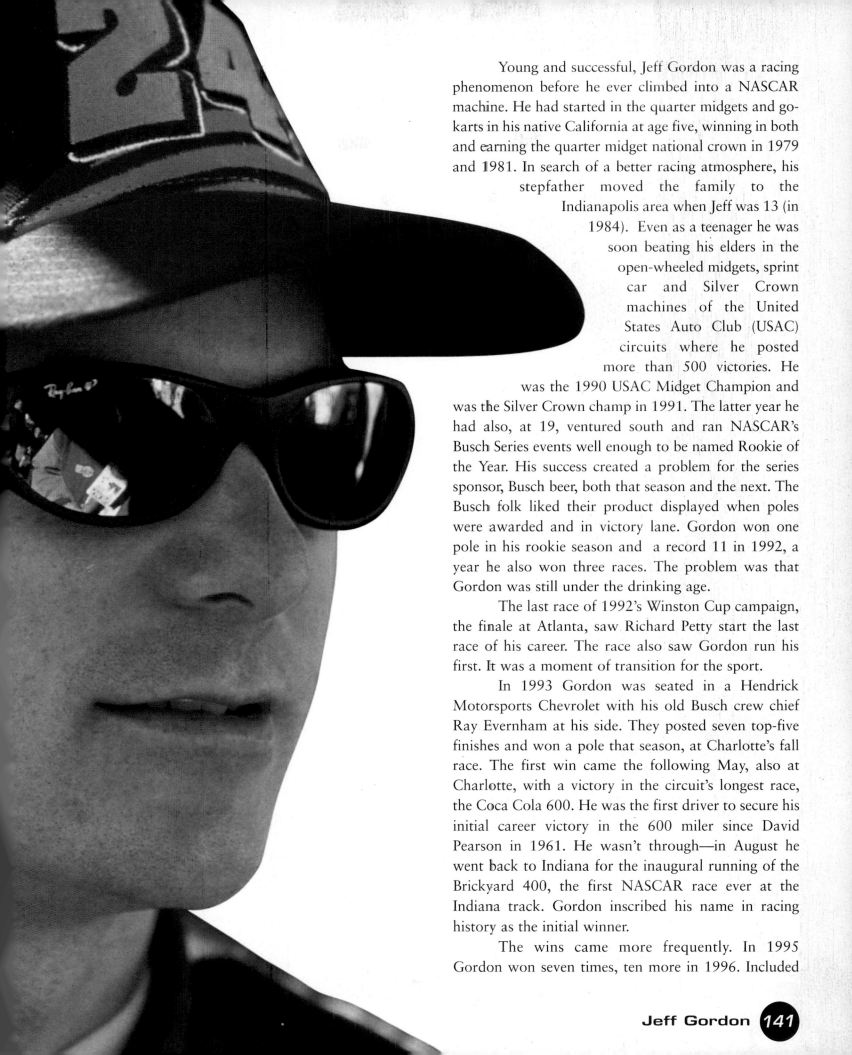

Young and successful, Jeff Gordon was a racing phenomenon before he ever climbed into a NASCAR machine. He had started in the quarter midgets and go-karts in his native California at age five, winning in both and earning the quarter midget national crown in 1979 and 1981. In search of a better racing atmosphere, his stepfather moved the family to the Indianapolis area when Jeff was 13 (in 1984). Even as a teenager he was soon beating his elders in the open-wheeled midgets, sprint car and Silver Crown machines of the United States Auto Club (USAC) circuits where he posted more than 500 victories. He was the 1990 USAC Midget Champion and was the Silver Crown champ in 1991. The latter year he had also, at 19, ventured south and ran NASCAR's Busch Series events well enough to be named Rookie of the Year. His success created a problem for the series sponsor, Busch beer, both that season and the next. The Busch folk liked their product displayed when poles were awarded and in victory lane. Gordon won one pole in his rookie season and a record 11 in 1992, a year he also won three races. The problem was that Gordon was still under the drinking age.

The last race of 1992's Winston Cup campaign, the finale at Atlanta, saw Richard Petty start the last race of his career. The race also saw Gordon run his first. It was a moment of transition for the sport.

In 1993 Gordon was seated in a Hendrick Motorsports Chevrolet with his old Busch crew chief Ray Evernham at his side. They posted seven top-five finishes and won a pole that season, at Charlotte's fall race. The first win came the following May, also at Charlotte, with a victory in the circuit's longest race, the Coca Cola 600. He was the first driver to secure his initial career victory in the 600 miler since David Pearson in 1961. He wasn't through—in August he went back to Indiana for the inaugural running of the Brickyard 400, the first NASCAR race ever at the Indiana track. Gordon inscribed his name in racing history as the initial winner.

The wins came more frequently. In 1995 Gordon won seven times, ten more in 1996. Included

both years were triumphs in the Southern 500 at Darlington, the oldest 500 in stock car history. His 1995 campaign resulted in Gordon, at 24 years of age, becoming the youngest driver to win the Winston Cup championship under the point system employed since 1975. The second youngest ever behind 1950 champion Bill Rexford, 23.

Only a handful of bad finishes during the 1996 campaign prevented him from winning a second straight crown e. It was a title he lost to his Hendrick team mate Terry Labonte by a mere 37 points.But Gordon was back even stronger in 1997. He started the season with a victory at Daytona, the first of ten victories. Again included was the venerable Darlington event. He went into the race with Daytona 500 and Coca Cola 600 victories. A win in the Labor Day classic would get him the Winston $1 million bonus. It had been won only once, by Bill Elliott in 1985. He won the race and the million. It was an unprecedented third straight triumph in NASCAR's oldest super speedway event. In 49 years, since its 1950 inaugural, no driver had ever won three straight. Not the sport's pioneers, the drivers of the 1970s or 1980s nor the current crop.

Gordon won other races that season and completed his resume by winning on a road course (Watkins Glen) en route to his second Winston Cup title in three seasons. He compiled a 1997 record of 10 more wins. In 1998, Gordon again led the circuit in poles (7), victories (13) and his third crown. The 50th anniversary season for Winston Cup, 1999, found Gordon leading the circuit with seven victories and as many poles the DNFs (Did Not Finish) cost him a shot at being just the second driver in race history to take the title three straight seasons. Three more wins were to follow in 2000. In 2001 he won his fourth title, helped by six victories, and $6,649,076 in money won.

In just nine seasons he has amassed 40 poles, 58 wins and over $45 million in career earnings. Jeff Gordon was a phenom before he got to NASCAR. His incredible record since has not altered that perception.

A life-long resident of the small mountain community of Stuart, Virginia, Glen Wood's early life revolved around the lumber business. As a youth he spent his time when not in school cutting trees from the heavily timbered countryside and hauling logs to area sawmills. It was an area rich in natural resources and also noted for illicit alcohol production.

Although never a part of the latter industry, young Glen was fascinated by the cars used in it. They were fast and could negotiate the twisting roads of the area smoothly despite the heavy

Glen Wood

Winner of 92 races as a team owner

liquid loads. He studied how the cars were built and prepared. It was information he would apply in future years.

Wood was just 20 years old when World War Two ended, and shortly afterwards racing resumed. A track had been built at nearby Martinsville and races were being run at the quarter-mile around the football field at Bowman-Grey Stadium just down the road at Winston Salem, North Carolina. He went to those events and watched with interest. He saw somethging he wanted to be a part of.

He finally obtained a car, a former police car which had been wrecked during the pursuit of a whiskey hauler. He repaired it and was soon the scourge of area tracks. Even Glen doesn't recall how many of the races his Modified car won, but his rivals ruefully racall it was in the hundreds.

The thrill of competition, even winning, at that level did not satisfy the mountain youth. He wanted more and found it in the new car circuit recently begun by NASCAR under the Grand National banner.

Glen Wood made his first start in NASCAR's major league in 1953. In his 11 seasons as a driver he started 62 races and won four. He also won 14 pole positions, led 15 of those races and had over half of his starts, 35, result in a top-ten finish. The record is more impressive when you consider during four of those years Wood concentrated his efforts in NASCAR's Convertible Division.

Running the "rag-tops", Wood was in 88 races and scored five wins. Nearly half of his starts, 42, saw a top-five finish, two thirds in the top ten.

Wood's strangest top five came in September 1965 at the half-mile Asheville–Weaverville Speedway in North Carolina's mountains. He had qualified his

The Wood brothers set the standard for teamwork

topless Ford on the outside of the front row in the 24-car field. With less than 20 of the 200 laps remaining Wood was running third when a wreck started on the backstretch. Before it concluded in the third turn all but one of the cars on the track had been involved and were through for the day. Curtis Turner, who had seen the wreck start in his rear-view mirror while leading, was the only driver to escape the mechanical carnage and was declared the winner. Wood was credited with third place.

With the 1959 opening of the Daytona International Speedway, the inaugural Daytona 500 was listed as a "Sweepstakes" race, one open to both hardtops and convertibles. Wood entered on the topless side and won the pole position for his class. The preliminaries saw 100-mile qualifying races for each group. Wood led the first lap and was also in front as the field took the white silk's "One Lap To Go" signal. But he was then made the victim of the track's first freight train pass as three cars swept by him in the final circuit. (The average speed for the 100 miles was 129.219mph, faster than Wood's 128.810 pole speed.)

Wood drove his last race in 1964 and teamed up with his brother Leonard and other family members to form the Wood brothers team which has scored 92 victories with drivers like Marvin Panch, Cale Yarborough, David Pearson, A.J. Foyt, Neil Bonnett and Curtis Turner. All of Wood's drivers on that list share a place with Glen on NASCAR's list of their top 50 drivers on the organization's first 50 years.

Bob Welborn

Seven-time race-winner in the Winston Cup

Grand National Division (now Winston Cup) had run 76 races in 1955. NASCAR president Bill France knew he couldn't make more days, so he chose to add a division, the Convertibles, to his inventory of products to afford NASCAR races to more tracks.

While Curtis Turner won the new group's first three races, Welborn soon came to the fore and became the second winner in rag-top competition under the NASCAR banner. His initial victory came at a paved one-third mile track on April 8, 1956 in Fayetteville, North Carolina, not far from his home in Denton. Welborn would go on to win 18 more times in his 111 races. He scored an amazing 87 top-ten finishes (nearly 80 per cent) in those events.

Welborn's consistent performances led to his winning the division's championship for the first three years of its existence. It was a feat not equaled in Winston Cup until two decades later when Cale Yarborough won the circuit's championships in 1976, 1977 and 1978.

The convertible circuit began to fade during the 1958 season. Welborn saw the trend and transferred much of his focus to the Winston Cup division. When Daytona International Speedway prepared for its inaugural 1959 Daytona 500, Welborn went, but there was a roof on his car now. He took the event's inaugural pole position with a run of 140.121mph—an unprecedented speed for stock cars in the late 1950s. He would go on to win the 100-mile qualifying race and become the track's first Winston Cup winner. (The qualifying races were points events until 1972.) In that first-ever Daytona 500, Welborn became its first lap leader, too, before being sidelined by mechanical failure near the event's mid-way point.

At the inaugural Daytona 500 in 1959 he took the first pole position and went on to become the track's first Winston Cup winner

Welborn won three times that season with his final triumph coming at the half-mile track in Weaverville, North Carolina in August. It was his ninth and last career win.

He raced sporadically over five more seasons, still stacking up solid top-five and top-ten finishes, but the zest for competition was gone. He quietly retired from the sport to his North Carolina home and was inducted in the National Motorsports Hall of Fame in 1982.

He often visited the garage areas at tracks after his induction as he gamely fought a battle with cancer. It was a fight he lost in 1997, prior to being named as one of the greatest drivers of NASCAR's first 50 years.

Although he spent little time in NASCAR's major league, the circuit now known as the Winston Cup Series, Ralph Earnhardt was named on the list of NASCAR's best of the first 50 years. His prowess was not in the new cars which dominated the publicity and garnered the bulk of attention. Earnhardt's forte lay in the dirt-track bull rings of NASCAR's Late Model Sportsman division which later became its Busch Grand National Division.

Ralph Earnhardt

Master of the dirt-track bull rings

Racing out of the shop which later became his home in Kannapolis, North Carolina, the slender Earnhardt loved the competition of racing where the car was broadsliding most of the time. He was a master at taking a car quickly down the straightway and pitching it sideways as he approached the turn. Once the car was cocked, he would stab the gas pedal and power slide through the corner. It was an art he developed through his years of such racing. Some claim the wily veteran was among the very best in the entire country.

He was certainly good enough to earn the 1956 championship of the Late Model Sportsman circuit, a crown that required towing his tattered coupe to tracks up and down the eastern seaboard and having time to work on it while running four or five nights a week. Although records are sketchy, he is thought to have won several hundreds of heat and feature races during those barnstorming seasons. His skill and talent were sufficient to be offered a ride in one of the potent DePaolo Racing factory-backed Fords toward the end of the 1956 campaign in NASCAR's major league.

Ralph Earnhardt won hundreds of career short-track races and the Late Model Sportsman title in 1956

The offer came for the November 11 race at the four-tenths mile-dirt track at Hickory, North Carolina, the 55th event of the season's 56-race schedule. It was a track where Earnhardt had won many times and he utilized his "home field" knowledge to the fullest. Although the car was strange, he promptly took it to the pole position in time trials in his first major league start. He showed the time trial run was not a fluke by also leading the race. It was an event which found him in second place at the end, behind only the white Chrysler 300 fielded by Carl Kiekhaefer and piloted by Alfred "Speedy" Thompson.

Earnhardt was most at home on the short tracks, but displayed an affinity for the larger "super speedways" as well. In the second season of racing at the 1.5-mile Charlotte Super Speedway, track management decided to hold 100-mile qualifying races to set the field for 1961's World 600. It was a program similar to the qualifying heat which set the line-up at Daytona's 500-mile winter classic. Ford's Fred Lorenzen was the best in time trials and had the pole for the first 100. Starting third in the field was Earnhardt in a Cotton Owens Pontiac.

Lorenzen led the first 50 miles, but taking command from him came the white Pontiac piloted by Earnhardt. He stayed in front for the next nine laps before relinquishing the lead to young Richard Petty's only Charlotte victory for the next 14 seasons.

Despite the taste of the big time, Earnhardt returned to the short track battles where he continued to win with only occasional forays in the big league. He preferred the shorter travel Sportsman competition that gave him more time at home with his wife Martha and their children. Among the latter was a skinny son, their first born, who had been named after him: Ralph Dale Earnhardt. The youngster would follow his father's tire tracks to the short tracks and later onto the sport's big time where he dropped the Ralph and became known as "The Intimidator" Dale Earnhardt.

Sadly Ralph never got to see his son's success in the major league. He died of a heart attack while working on his car in the shop behind his home in 1973, seven years before Dale won his first Winston Cup championship.

Red Farmer

A 700-plus victory career

As he nears his 70th birthday, you might still see him power-sliding his car around the red-clay corners of Alabama

He tired of racing at the same tracks and against the same adversaries every week and looked for new worlds where he could test his skills. Migrating northwesterly, Farmer found fertile fields in the Birmingham area. He set up shop in Hueytown and sent word back to Miami about the great competition he had found at tracks in Birmingham, Nashville, Montgomery and Mobile. He was first followed to the new venues by another Miami youth named Bobby Allison, and then by Allison's younger brother, Donnie.

The moves were the beginning of the famed "Alabama Gang". When the trio rolled into tracks in Tennessee, Georgia and Florida, it wasn't unusual to hear the local speedmerchants bemoan, "Oh oh. Here comes that Alabama Gang." And the gang, led by Farmer, gave locals reason to dread their arrival. The trio won regularly in both Modified and Sportsman events.

Farmer was the first to spread out. in 1956 he traveled all over the eastern part of the country with his strong Modified machine and wound up as the National Champion. It would be the first of four titles the red head would win under the NASCAR banner.

As the Modified circuit became more concentrated in the northeast quadrant of the country as the 1950s waned, Farmer and most other southern racers switched their focus to the rapidly growing Late Model Sportsman division. It was the circuit which came to dominate the weekly racing at the myriad tracks that dotted the southeast.

Farmer had found a new home, and came to be the dominant driver in that division, too, as the 1960s faded into the 1970s. He won there, too, and often. He won the LMS championship for the first time in 1969 and would take the crown again for the next two years.

Even though none of Farmer's 700-plus NASCAR wins came in the Winston Cup division races, he is still acclaimed as one of the best short track drivers in the sanctioning body's history. It is the kind of racing he still enjoys as he nears his 70th birthday. Often on a Saturday night on a dirt track in Alabama you might find him still power sliding his car through the red clay corners and smiling as he does it. Sometimes, too, although not as often as in prior years, you might still see him adding to his long, long list of racing victories.

Nearly as old as NASCAR, Red Farmer still wins

W

When Ray Hendrick came to a race track, he came to win. Racing terms like "charger", "intimidator" and even "legend" apply to only a handful of drivers. But they are all true descriptions of the bear of a man from Richmond, Virginia, who laughed easily and could run the wheels off a race car.

In a career that lasted over 30 years, and began in the mid-1950s, Hendrick is estimated to have won over 700 times. "We'd win 35 to 40 races a year," Hendrick said. "But there were no records kept when I first started."

Typical of his success were his 20 victories at Martinsville, 13 in Modified events and seven in Late

The man who came to win

Ray Hendrick

Model Sportsman (now Busch Grand National). It is a record that still stands. He won his last race at the track in 1975.

And he raced against the best, from the likes of Ralph Earnhardt, Joe Weatherly, Tim and Fonty Flock, Glen Wood and Perk Brown in the early days to Richie Evans, Jerry Cook, Bugs Stevens, Fred De Sarro and Geoff and Bret Bodine in the latter phase of his driving career.

The fans called him "Mr Modified", and voted him NASCAR's Most Popular Modified Driver in 1969. The title was appropriate because he won on nearly every track, large and small, from Florida to Maine. It was more than likely that his competition called him other names, too, but they still knew that he was the man to beat.

While Hendrick was always a flat-out, fire-breathing charger, he still had a close relationship with the man he loved to beat.

In 1961 he was selected as NASCAR's Sportsman of the Year for his conduct on the track. The act that clinched the coveted award came at a race at his hometown Fairgrounds track.

A car driven by Emanual Zervakis hit the fence in the first turn and did a complete flip on its side, squarely in front of the pack that was thundering toward the dazed driver.

Hendrick whipped his car sideways to a stop and used it as a shield to protect Zervakis. The field got by safely. While Bobby Isaac won the race, Zervakis and the fans knew Hendrick was the real winner of the day.

While he drove for such car owners as John Tadlock and Dick Armstrong, Hendrick enjoyed his greatest success with Jack Tant and Clay Mitchell in their red "Flying Eleven" Modified Chevrolet coupe and later a Late Model Sportsman car with the same color and number. In 11 Martinsville races from 1968 through 1971, the talented combination won eight of them.

Hendrick became so dominant there that for the 1971 spring 100-lapper, promotor H. Clay Earles decided to invert the field to see if Hendrick could be beaten. He naturally won the pole, good for 33rd and last starting position, and proceeded to pass all 32 cars for yet another victory.

At the Martinsville oval he won 50-lappers, 100-lappers, 500-lappers and when the track launched its double headers in 1970, Hendrick swept both the 250-lap Modifed race and the 250-lap Late Sportsman feature.

And while Hendrick virtually owned Martinsville, he also scored at such speedways as Langhorne, Trenton, Pocono, Charlotte and Talladega. One of his hottest rivalries was with NASCAR Modified champion, Carl "Bugs" Stevens.

"That sumbitchin Bugsy is a hard guy to beat," Hendrick said. "He's my kinda race driver."

Hendrick, a member of the National Motorsports Hall of Fame, ran the toughest race of his career against cancer, and battled it for four years before succumbing on September 28, 1990, at the age of 61. Appropriately he was buried in his driver's uniform. Ray Hendrick always came to win. And he usually did.

More than 500 wins in Modified and Late Model Sportsman Divisions

Jack Ingram came on to the scene in Busch Grand National racing in the early 1970s when the NASCAR division was still known as the Late Model Sportsman circuit. It was a time when the drivers had to be tough, and that was a description which fit the stockily built former pipe-fitter. Before he hung up his helmet he had earned the deserved title as the division's "Iron Man" for his steely will and dogged determination on the tracks.

A native of the North Carolina mountains around his home town of Asheville, Ingram was a stalwart of the

Jack Ingram

The "Iron Man" of the Busch scene

circuit on tracks up and down the east coast of the country. He competed and won at tracks like Hickory and South Boston, Daytona, Milwaukee, Oxford, Maine and Darlington, South Carolina.

Before the name was changed and the Busch Series became a touring division, the Late Model Sportsmen competitors ran at weekly tracks. To win the championship you had to either be very good at a few tracks or hustle around the country and win at a wide variety of circuits. In the early 1970s Ingram chose the latter path and was able to amass a record which earned him the division's crown for three straight years (1972–1974).

When the change came in 1982, Ingram was equally at home. He had run the tracks where the Busch Series competed while barnstorming a decade earlier and became the first Busch Series champion after it evolved to tour status with no "home" track. It was a title he would win again in 1985, the year he scored a season high, tying five victories in the 27 races.

The 1985 crown was the fifth Ingram had won in the second-most popular division of NASCAR racing. He retired at the end of the decade as the only five-time champion in the 40-year history of the division under either name.

None of the crowns was won easily, although he wore them well. His first, in 1972, came after running in 86 events. He won 15 of them. The following season he won 11 of the 18 national championship events he started and amassed points in weekly races to also finish high in the standings of three different states.

Ingram was an innovator, too. His 1985 title run included a victory that fall at North Carolina's North Wilkesboro Speedway when his Chevy was powered by a V-6. It made him the first driver in the division's history to win an event with that type of engine.

Nearly all of Ingram's career was dedicated to the competition in the LMS-Busch circuit. He did venture into the world of Winston Cup in 19 races. Usually his role was to fill in for an ill or injured major league star. His best run came, however, in 1967, when he drove his own car in a race at Hickory, North Carolina. It was a track where he won eight times in his normal competition. He qualified sixth and went on to a career-best second place finish to winner Richard Petty.

When Ingram retired from driving in the late-1980s he left the Busch circuit with a record 31 victories in 275 starts after the division's 1982 conversion. His record stood nearly a decade before being broken in late 1997 by Mark Martin.

Broad shouldered and quiet, Jack Ingram may have been known as his circuit's "Iron Man", but his skill as a driver was pure gold.

The only five-time champion in the 40-year history of the division under either of the circuit's names

Richie Evans had a passion for modification and for being a top driver at all times. "My heart is in this," Evans said bluntly. "In fact I want to win. I'll admit that I'm a sore loser, but I think before it's too far a race loser is not a good winner. I'd rather get to the point where I could win it all."

The love that Evans, along the low bracket Modified division dares to be blessed two top former American Hall of fame, won the annual championship nine times any other has won in the field of NASCAR safely.

Never was consistent the legendary Modified driver, the nine time crowned to conduct by of old time driver Richie Evans...

Richie Evans

Modified Division winner of nine titles

during a career which produced well over 400 victories.

He won mostly on short tracks where the Modified Division normally raced. But he also won the 1979 event and the following year took the final race for the division run on the huge 2.5-mile Daytona International Speedway.

From 1978 through 1985, Evans won an unprecedented eight straight titles and the orange number 61 became the car to beat. One of his keys to success was designing and building his own cars.

"Working with the car and working on it in the garage every week is an advantage," he said. "While I'm working on the car, I'm thinking about every lap I rode in that thing. It's not like the mechanic who stood and watched it during the feature and then has to make some decisions.

"I can sit there and think every lap out and look at the lap chart from the whole race to see what's going on and what I am feeling and then make an adjustment."

Evans became so dominant in a six-year span, from 1978 through 1983, he won 200 races. He took 25 in 1978, 52 in 1979, 37 in 1980, 38 in 1981, 23 in 1982 and 32 during the final year of the span.

In a sensational 1979 campaign, 37 of his wins came in 60 starts and he finished in the top five an astounding 54 times.

At Martinsville Speedway, a showcase for the division, Evans won ten times, second only to Ray Hendrick's 13, and won in what speedway founder H. Clay Earles called "The greatest finish of any race, anywhere".

In 1981's spring Modified race, Evans and Geoff Bodine had endured a race-long battle for the win. Coming out of the fourth turn on the final lap on their way to the checkered flag, they tangled. Both cars went into the outer concrete wall. Their tires got a bit on the cement and climbed the barrier. The impact sheared a wheel off Evans's car and sent Bodine's mount careering across the track and into the pit road wall. Spinning, smoking and showering sparks, the two drivers stayed on the gas. Evans, on three wheels, bounced across the finish line first.

Typical of Evans's career was his last season in which the Modified title was decided in a 29-race schedule. Before the final race of the season, at Martinsville, he had won a dozen times, finished among the top five 17 times and was in the top ten 21 times to clinch his ninth title.

His nine Modified Division titles included eight straight championships (1978–85)

He was fatally injured when his car crashed headlong into the wall between the third and fourth turns in the initial practice session of the event.

Evans went out a winner. He never reached the point where he had to quit.

Jerry Cook, now Competition Administrator for NASCAR, is the perfect man for the job. He knows about competition first hand. The former race driver from Rome, New York was the national champion of NASCAR's early rough-and-tumble Modified Division six times, including four years in a row from 1974–1977.

Cook not only won the division's crown six times, he finished second in the season's dogfight another half dozen years and was third in the hunt in two other campaigns.

The Modified Division actually is an evolvement from NASCAR's early days when the late Red Byron drove to

Jerry Cook

Six-time Modified Division winner

His six titles came in a seven-year span

victory in the sanctioning body's first race on the Beach and Road course in Florida. In the inaugural 1948 season it was known as the "Modified Stock Division".

Cook was a full-time racer in the Modified ranks and never sought to move up to the Winston Cup ranks although the offers were there. "I could make more money in that division at that time than in the big one," he recalls.

His modified 1975 Pinto, powered by a 439 cubic inch Chevrolet engine, cranked out some 650 horsepower. Being the champ made him a drawing card. It sometimes made him a target, too.

"I wouldn't doubt that some drivers got carried away trying to beat me because I was the champion," Cook says with a smile. "I was knocked out of the races two or three times a year."

Cook started tinkering with cars when he was just ten years old and built his own by the time he was 13. He made his racing debut at 16 "going from first to last in about two laps", on a quarter-mile track. "I didn't win the pole, either," Cook laughed, "because the car that had won the least money started up front."

By the time he turned 19, Cook was the owner of a Modified car with someone else behind the wheel, but finally took over the driving duties himself. "I figured I might as well drive it if I was going to have to fix it all the time. My driver completely totalled two cars in one year."

Cook went on the tour full-time in 1963 and, unlike most of the division's drivers who held full-time jobs outside the sport, his business was racing. And business was good. He won seven times at Martinsville Speedway's half-mile

oval, the site of the division's biggest events in the 1970s.

"Often, there were several races on any given weekend," Cook explained. "That meant drivers were split up, and not all the top ones got to the same track. But when we came to Martinsville, everyone was there. There were at least 15 cars there in every race who could win."

To find competition Cook didn't have to go far from his hometown. Rome, New York was a city of residence he shared with another Modified division super star, Richie Evans. Between the two they brought the "Mod Squad's" championship trophy back to their community for 15 straight years (1971–1985).

What began as tinkering for a kid, became a hobby then an avocation and an occupation in a career that landed Jerry Cook in the National Motorsports Hall of Fame.

Young Guns

While much of this book focuses on the first half-century of NASCAR's history we would be remiss by not looking ahead with a focus on the new faces who may succeed some of the 50 drivers described in these pages.

Since the 1998 season, there have been 11 drivers breaking into the ranks as Winston Cup winners, including a modern-day record five new winners during the 2001 campaign. Among them they accounted for 29 victories in the 104 races contested in the three seasons. And there are a host of others who may join them among the elite who win in the most competitive form of motorsports on earth.

Not included among the top 50 of the first 50 years is Bobby Labonte, younger brother of Terry and the 2000 champion. His title, and 18 race

victories, makes the Corpus Christi natives the first set of siblings to ever claim NASCAR's top crown. Nor is his teammate at Joe Gibbs Racing, Tony Stewart. The Indiana native and former open wheel champion has won a dozen Cup races and was second in the 2001 points chase to Jeff Gordon.

Another set of brothers, Jeff and Ward Burton from South Boston, Virginia, have already posted 20 victories between them and could well be major contenders for inclusion among the top 50 drivers in NASCAR's second half-century.

Steve Park, a second-generation NASCAR competitor, afforded Dale Earnhardt Inc. its initial victory when he won the 2000 Watkins Glen race in his native New York and Michael Waltrip added a Daytona 500 victory to the team's laurels to open the 2001 season as he finished just ahead of his DEI teammate, Dale Earnhardt, Jr. Tragically the victory was marred by the death of the team owner who crashed on the event's final lap while his cars led the way to the checkered flag.

The death of the elder Earnhardt, ranked by many as one of the very best to ever grip a steering wheel, left a huge void in the sport and at Richard Childress Racing, for whom he drove. Tapped as his successor at the controls of the GM Goodwrench Chevrolet by Childress was young Kevin Harvick who had already been signed to drive for the team on the full Busch circuit. The young Californian promptly affirmed the choice by nosing out Jeff Gordon for a victory at Atlanta in just his third Cup start. He went on to win the inaugural event at the new Chicagoland Speedway and finish ninth in the season's points (despite not starting the season opener) and take Winston Cup Rookie of the Year honors. He did all of this while also running the full Busch Series schedule and winning the championship for the Childress team.

Harvick's Busch title followed two consecutive claims to that crown by the young Earnhardt whose grandfather Ralph Earnhardt had claimed the same crown in the mid-1950s when it was known as NASCAR's Sportsman division and whose father had taken the Winston Cup championship a record tying seven times. Those feats make the Earnhardt family the only one in all of NASCAR's history to have three generations of champions.

With his father's death young Earnhardt was pushed into a leadership role at DEI, a load he carried well. During the 2000 season he scored his breakthrough victory at Texas and backed it up with a win that fall at the three-quarter mile Richmond track. The 2001 campaign found the young North Carolinian winning when the teams returned to Daytona for the July 400-mile classic and adding triumphs at Dover and Talladega in the fall. The five wins in his first two full seasons left him just one victory shy of what his famed father had accomplished during his first two years of competing on the full schedule of races.

While Earnhardt, Harvick, the Burtons, the younger Labonte and Stewart are among those who have emerged as bona fide stars on the scene, others hover on the periphery. Young talents like Casey Atwood, Kevin Busch, Penske protégé Ryan Newman, Jeff Gordon's selection of Jimmie Johnson and youthful Stuart Kirby are among those many see as the future stars. Only time and the whims of racing luck will determine the accuracy of the forecasts in the opening of NASCAR's second 50 years.

The Teams

No driver can win a race without a car. They also need the backing, preparation, and service of a talented crew. In its first **50** years, the major **NASCAR** circuit has had many teams who had the right combination of those traits to be truly successful.

DePaolo Engineering

In 1956, Ford Motor Company determined it would get serious about stock car racing. To do so, they named 1925 Indianapolis 500 winner Peter DePaolo to head their program under a DePaolo Engineering name plate. The stocky, mustachioed Italian selected Ralph Moody and Fireball Roberts as his drivers.

The team's first appearance came in the February race on the beach-road circuit in Daytona, with Moody bringing his motor home in third but Roberts dropping out with mechanical woes. It was a small start but built to success as Roberts won five times and Moody contributed four more wins in the initial season that saw West Coast stars Bill Amick and Bill Carden added to the stable, and had Joe Weatherly and Curtis Turner competing in the Convertible division. Turner put DePaolo's topless Ford in victory lane 22 times in their 57-race campaign, while Weatherly added four victories.

In 1957, DePaolo added Marvin Panch and Ralph Earnhardt to the team now overseen by John Holman, a gravel-voiced mechanic with a keen business acumen. The team was even stronger as the new season opened. Panch won the first two races and the team, led by Roberts, swept the top four spots in the third. It was a feat they would repeat again at North Wilkesboro and remains unmatched by an owner. Turner, Weatherly and Roberts won 14 of the opening 21 Convertible events. Moody, Panch, Roberts, and new driver Paul Goldsmith won ten of the season's first 16 Grand National races before the bottom dropped out.

In early June 1957, all the factories got out of racing, Ford included. They gave the drivers a race car, tow truck, and tools. Moody hocked his airplane to buy the surplus parts and equipment, coupling with Holman to form an even more successful team. Holman and Moody cars featured a driver list reading like a Stock Car Hall of Fame roster: Roberts, Weatherly, Turner, Fred Lorenzen, Nelson Stacy, David Pearson, and Bobby Allison won 57 races at tracks on the Winston Cup circuit and a dozen more on tracks which stood where shopping malls now exist. Pearson won the driving crown for them in 1968 and 1969, with 27 victories over the two seasons.

The famed H-M logo faded from the scene as they quit fielding teams when the sport entered the 1970s, but the legacy of the organization and excellence they represented impacts the teams of the 1990s.

Hendrick Motorsports

In 1984, a car dealer and former boat drag racer named Rick Hendrick decided he wanted to go stock car racing in NASCAR's major league. He hired veteran crew chief Harry Hyde to build his team and tagged modified stand-out and Late Model winner Geoff Bodine to be his driver. The team came together quickly as they won their eighth start together at Martinsville, Virginia. That victory marked the emergence of Hendrick Motorsports.

The task wasn't easy. They had to beat the established and successful teams to succeed: groups like Junior Johnson's stable, the Fords of Bud Moore and Harry Melling, and fellow Chevy owner Richard Childress.

By the 1986 campaign, Hendrick was fielding a two-car team with Bodine and brash newcomer Tim Richmond behind the wheels, while expanding his shops and adding mechanical talent. They won nine of the year's 29 events. By 1987, Hendrick was sending as many as five cars to races. Star drivers Darrell Waltrip and Benny Parsons were seated in the Hendrick mounts and everyone knew the talented teams would have to be reckoned with. Hendrick built his racing organization with the same skills he had utilized to bring his far flung dealerships to prominence in the country: through acute business senses, attracting talented people, and strong sponsorship support.

Quick to recognize talent and with 32 victories to his credit by the end of the 1992 campaign, Hendrick was able to lure sprint car and midget ace Jeff Gordon out of the Busch Series ranks and away from the Ford camp and into his Chevrolets. Gordon quickly became a winner and by 1995 was Hendrick's first Winston Cup Champion. It was a thrill Hendrick felt again in 1996 as Terry Labonte took the crown in a season-ending battle between Labonte and Gordon. It marked only the second time in the sport's history any owner has won consecutive titles with different drivers and the first time it had happened in nearly 40 seasons.

The Hendrick Motorsports teams won 22 of the 62 races during the 1995–1996 seasons, a dominant number, through shared technology and skilled personnel on both sides of the pit wall and in their three shops. In four of the 1996 events, Hendrick cars finished one-two.

Although diagnosed with a rare bone marrow cancer after the 1996 season, Hendrick had his biggest thrill in the 1997 season-opening Daytona 500, as he watched his trio of cars take the top three spots in the nationally televised event.

In 2001 Jeff Gordon gave the recovered Hendrick his fifth title in seven years, lifting his Cup wins over the 100 mark while pushing his winnings to nearly $90 million.

Junior Johnson & Associates

Junior Johnson's Hall of Fame driving career ended when he last doffed his helmet at the end of the 1966 season. It was then he donned his car owner's headgear. In doing so, the portly North Carolina native began an equally storied career in the major league of American stock car racing.

His car, with Darrell Dieringer driving, convincingly won the first year out. At Johnson's home track, North Wilkesboro, Dieringer earned the pole position and proceeded to lead all 400 laps of the race. A few years later, Johnson's car did the same, with Cale Yarborough now in the seat, at

Bristol, Tennessee, where he commanded the field for all 500 circuits. It is the only time any driver led every lap on any of the tracks which have been part of the sport's modern era.

Between the two events' domination, Johnson cars were equally stout. In 1969, with LeeRoy Yarborough driving, the team won the Daytona 500, Charlotte's World 600, and Darlington's Southern 500—the biggest, longest, and oldest events on the big track schedule. The same feat today would have earned them the 'Winston $Million' and is something done just three times over the events' histories.

A great era for Johnson's teams came in the 1970s when Cale Yarborough handled the driving duties. It was an era which saw them win 55 races, 39 poles, and three consecutive (1976–78) Winston Cup championships, the latter a feat not duplicated before or since.

Johnson teamed with Charlotte Motor Speedway head Richard Howard in 1971 to bring a competitive Chevrolet back to the circuit. They succeeded by winning the pole for Charlotte's 600-miler and winning the fastest race in the history of Bristol's oval, both with 'Chargin' Charlie Glotzbach as driver.

The following year, the Howard-owned, Johnson-managed Chevy had Bobby Allison driving to ten wins in 31 starts, with a dozen more second place finishes. They started on the front row in 19 of those races, including 11 pole positions. They were the car to beat as they led the first 30 races of that 1971 season's 30 events.

Wishing to reduce his schedule, Yarborough left Johnson and was quickly succeeded by a brash youngster from Tennessee named Darrell Waltrip. Displaying the powerful potential of the team, they won a dozen races in each of their first two seasons together and took back-to-back championships for their efforts. They were still teamed in 1985 when The Winston All-Star race was first run. They were the inaugural winners and went on to win the World 600 the next day. That big weekend came in the midst of a super season by Bill Elliott, when he drove Harry Melling's Ford to the Winston $Million pay day for winning three of the circuit's big four events. But, at season's end, it was Johnson's car with Waltrip driving that won the 1985 championship, their third together.

As a car owner, Johnson had watched stoically as his vehicles won 139 times and earned six championships. But to the former moonshiner, it was no fun anymore. He retired again at the end of the '96 campaign, leaving the sport richer by his presence and with a record of success seldom found.

Carl Kiekhaefer

Obstinate, cantankerous, opinionated, tyrannical, peculiar, and dictatorial are words used to describe Carl Kiekhaefer of Fond Du Lac, Wisconsin's millionaire owner of Mercury Outboard Motors, who emerged on the stock car scene suddenly at the start of the 1955 season. Another term often assigned to his business and racing efforts is 'successful.' He was all of those, as well as being an innovator.

When NASCAR's major league arrived at the Daytona Beach road course for the first big event of their 1955 campaign, they faced a new entry. A gleaming Chrysler 300 with 'Mercury Outboards' emblazoned on its sides. No driver had been named to the mount but Kiekhaefer quickly signed Tim Flock, who had won the race a year earlier but quit NASCAR after being disqualified for a minor rules violation. The team clicked immediately. Flock drove 'Mr K's' big white car to 18 poles and an equal number of race wins (both thought unbeatable at the time) and the 1955 Series championship.

The Mercury team out-factoried the factories, first adding a second car driven by Tim's brother Fonty, and then a third with Alfred 'Speedy' Thompson behind the wheel. Each team had its own truck to transport it to the races in an era when most were driven or towed from race to race. Each crew of mechanics had uniforms, a bit of showmanship and professionalism unprecedented at the time. The irascible owner hired his own meteorologist to record weather factors and a geologist to sample and test the dirt of racing surfaces.

Kiekhaefer left no stone unturned in his drive to not only win but to dominate the sport. His cars won 22 of the 40 races they entered in 1955, with one-two finishes in four. In 11 of his 18 victories that season Tim Flock led every lap. For a 300-mile race at the 1.5-mile Le-Hi Speedway in West Memphis, Arkansas, Kiekhaefer entered four cars. All three Flock brothers—Tim, Fonty, and Bob—drove, plus AAA talent Norm Nelson, and he sponsored the other top contenders, even Ford factory teams from DePaolo Engineering. Speedy Thompson drove one of the latter to victory carrying the Mercury Outboard logo.

If the competition thought 1955 had been good for the 'K' cars, they hadn't seen anything. He came to Daytona

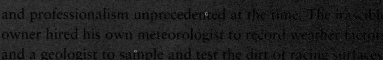

Mr K's cars dominated the sport in the 1950s

in 1956 with a five-car effort, having hired Buck Baker, Frank 'Rebel' Mundy and Charlie Scott (only the second Afro-American in the sport) to complement Tim Flock and Thompson. Flock gave him a second straight beach victory. His cars won 21 of the season's first 25 races. Flock suffered from ulcers and quit the team only to be replaced by Herb Thomas. The teams took 16 races in a row from March into May. Baker won 14 events that season and gave Kiekhaefer his second consecutive title, the first time in the sport's history anyone won straight owner titles with different drivers.

As suddenly as he had arrived, Kiekhaefer was gone. His frequent wins and domination of the sport resulted in boos of resentment from the fans. Fearing a negative effect on Mercury Outboard motor sales, the millionaire closed his racing shop and didn't return to a track until he was inducted into the sport's Hall of Fame at Darlington in 1980.

Petty Enterprises

To the inaugural 'Strictly Stock' at Charlotte in 1949, a farmer from central North Carolina brought the family Buick. He returned home chagrined. He had wrecked the car, rolling it in the race—the event's only mishap. His wife was not pleased with the results but Lee Petty was not deterred.

The incident was the start of a racing operation which has been the most successful in the history of the sport that became today's Winston Cup Series. Petty ran five more of the first season's races and would end up second in the standings at season's end only to champion Red Byron. All five of Petty's starts after the Charlotte debacle resulted in top ten finishes, including a win at Heidelburg Speedway in Pittsburgh. He thus established a pattern of success through consistent performance that became the foundation for Petty Enterprises.

Lee Petty's career launched a racing operation which has earned an unprecedented ten championships in

NASCAR's major circuit and recorded an unmatched 269 victories over the next 49 seasons. Included among the latter total are an enviable nine Daytona 500 victories, and the drivers who have won for the team are a Hall of Fame group. The latest additions to the list came from Bobby Hamilton's victories at Phoenix in 1996, Martinsville the following year and John Andretti's win at Phoenix in 1999.

The family store launched the career of Lee's son Richard toward his status as 'The King of Stock Car Racing'. It is a title earned by his 200 wins, seven driving crowns, and his seven visits to the Daytona 500 winners' circle where Lee Petty was the inaugural honoree following the event's initial running in 1959. It was under the Petty banner that Richard raced in the 1967 season when he set the single-season record of 27 victories, including ten consecutive, which is the only streak to exceed the mark set by Tim Flock in the Kiekhaefer Chryslers a dozen seasons earlier.

Before being severely injured in a Daytona 500 qualifying race in 1961, Lee had amassed 54 victories and three driving crowns. He was the series' first three-time champion, and might have earned it many more times but for being stripped of points a couple of seasons for competing in non-NASCAR races.

Other major races won by Petty machines included the 1964 600 at Charlotte, when Jim Paschal drove the team's second entry, and Marvin Panch's triumph in the same event two seasons later. Pete Hamilton won the 1970

Daytona 500 for Petty Enterprises and went on to sweep both of that season's events at the new Talladega Super Speedway in Alabama. The Petty cars, with Richard Plymouth-mounted and Buddy Baker in the team's Dodge, finished one-two in the 1971 Daytona 500, with Baker going on to give the organization yet a third victory in Charlotte's grueling 600-miler.

Lee Petty retired following his 1961 injuries. Richard hung up his helmet following the final event of the 1992 campaign. But Petty Enterprises continues as a long-lived and integral part of NASCAR big time circuits. Kyle Petty—Richard's son, Lee's grandson—races out of the team's shop, along with Buckshot Jones and Andretti, some four dozen seasons after the family car was flipped upside-down.

Raymond Parks

Even before NASCAR was formed in 1948, the cars of Atlanta's Raymond Parks were winners. Tall, thin, and dapper under his ever-present full-brimmed hat, Parks fielded the best teams in the fledgling days of stock car racing. He hired the best drivers, top mechanics, and gave them whatever it took to produce winning efforts on the dirt tracks of those early years.

Five races were held on the early beach-road circuit in Daytona in the two years after World War II. Parks' cars won all of them. His drivers included Roy Hall, Bob Flock and Red Byron during that period of 1946–47. Parks was part of the meeting in December 1947. His chief mechanic, Red Vogt, was there, too, and proposed the name for the organization—NASCAR. The new sanctioning body held its first race the next February on the hard-packed sands of Daytona. It was won by Byron in a car owned by Parks and prepared by Vogt. The team would go on to win the first championship under the organization's banner.

When NASCAR started its new car division in 1949, Parks' cars, prepared by Vogt and driven by Byron, were there. Although winning just twice, they finished well enough in the others to take the first championship for the Strictly Stock division which would become 'Grand National' the next season and grow to be today's Winston Cup Series.

While Byron was on his way to the inaugural crown for the new cars, Fonty Flock was busy winning the second straight Modified title in Parks' 1939 Ford. His success made him the first three-time championship owner and the only person of the sport's early era to win the titles of two NASCAR divisions in the same season.

The other victory Byron enjoyed in that precedent-setting 1949 campaign was his three-lap margin over Lee Petty in the circuit's inaugural event at Martinsville, Virginia's half-mile dirt oval. The triumph by Parks' Oldsmobile began a skein augmented by Ricky Craven's win on the same track in 2000 to extend the longest run of continuous racing in NASCAR major league.

The growth of the sport in those early days led to Parks' departure. The expanded circuits were taking his time from the Parks' Novelty Company he ran in Atlanta. His vending machines needed his attention—they were what had

provided his financial ability to field cars and support the sport. He is rumored to even have bankrolled a young race promoter named Bill France during some of the financially thin moments in the sport's infancy.

Parks left the sport with a legacy of class, some nice trophies, and a room full of memories he maintains in his Atlanta offices four decades after his significant contributions.

Richard Childress Racing

The route to heading a successful team takes many paths. For Richard Childress it started by selling peanuts, as a kid, at the Bowman-Grey Stadium track in his native Winston Salem, North Carolina. He watched the local stars battle in modified cars and thrilled when NASCAR's major drivers came to race on the eight-quarter-mile oval twice a year. Before long he was tinkering on cars at local shops, then driving on the track which circled the stadium's football field.

His skills honed, he moved into the big time of stock car racing in 1972 as owner/driver with only childhood friend Tim Brewer to help. They raced for seven years and developed into one of the top independent teams before deciding Childress' best talent lay in organizing the operation. During his struggling effort, he gradually built his team in the image of the highly successful pattern established by his childhood hero, Junior Johnson.

With the days of successful independent teams rapidly fading, in mid-1981 Childress tapped another promising youngster who had also grown up in racing, Dale Earnhardt. Together they ran the final 11 events of the campaign, but at season's end Earnhardt was lured to the factory-aided Bud Moore team. Childress saw promise in Moore's driver, Ricky Rudd, and signed him as his driver for the next two seasons. The combo tasted their first victory at Riverside (California) Raceway in June, 1983. They won again that Fall at Martinsville, Virginia. Childress found the success he'd hoped for. Moore and Childress exchanged drivers again following the 1983 campaign. With Earnhardt in the car and Childress calling the shots, the success came quickly with wins at the huge Talladega track in Alabama and on the demanding mile and a half Atlanta oval. They have stayed to win races every season since.

Well staffed, equipped, and sponsored, the Richard Childress Racing company became the team to beat in every race and for every championship. The latter is a goal they have achieved six times in the 1980s and 90s. Each time the crowns of champion driver and owner have come back-to-back. They took their first title together in 1986 and repeated the next season. They were the best in the sport again in 1990 and 1991 and again in 1993 and 1994.

The Childress-Earnhardt combination was separarted only by Earnhardt's death in 2001. Kevin Harvick was tapped as the successor and posted a top ten finish in the Winston Cup final point standings.

During the course of their association Earnhardt left his moniker all over the champion and winner tables. Part of that success came from fast and efficient pit work by the Childress staff, enabling the team to win over $54 million.

Dale Earnhardt Incorporated

The year 1982 was the starting point for two major parts of NASCAR's evolution. That was the year that saw the reorganization of NASCAR's Sportsman division into a new league under the Busch Grand National title. That year also found a new team formed by Dale and Teresa Earnhardt. They dubbed it Dale Earnhardt Inc., and aimed it for competition in the new circuit, winning the division's inaugural race at Daytona.

Over the next dozen years, while running a limited schedule of selected events, the team won 21 races and proved a formidable foe in most of the others. They won the Daytona 300 six more times including five consecutive (1990-1994) for a string unmatched before or since in the prestigious annual opening event.

The team's success led to the formation of an ambitious plan to expand their involvement in the three major NASCAR divisions: Busch, Craftsman Truck and, eventually, Winston Cup. By 1995 the Earnhardts were ready to implement. They picked Kentucky's Jeff Green for the Busch team and veteran Ron Hornaday as chauffeur for the entry into the new truck competition. Hornaday won pole for the division's inaugural race while Green posted top ten finishes in over half of his starts. The following season Hornaday won DEI its first NASCAR championship.

Steve Park, a Modified division standout from New York, was hand picked to succeed Green in 1997 and finished third in Busch points with three victories while Hornaday, en-route to winning a season high seven races, was signed to a long term agreement in the truck series. The scene was set for the final phase of DEI's expansion.

Park and the team moved up to the Winston Cup ranks for the 1998 season. Dale Earnhardt Jr, filled the Busch seat vacated by Park and Hornaday was geared for another run at the Truck title. Both Earnhardt, Jr. and Hornaday were successful in the championship bids but Park was injured at Atlanta. However three-time Cup champion Darrell Waltrip was slotted as Park's fill-in and provided the fledgling team its first top ten and top five finishes.

The 1999 campaign found Earnhardt, Jr. on his way to a second straight Busch title. DEI also made the decision to field a car, sponsored by Budweiser, in five Cup events, for the talented third generation driver. The team was now geared for a full run in 2000 where they won their first Cup events at Texas and Richmond. Park, meanwhile, gave his team a victory on the twisting Watkins Glen layout in his native state. Emphasis shifted to fielding a third team into Cup racing for 2001 with Michael Waltrip as the driver for the new NAPA Chevrolet team.

The three-car effort was an immediate success but came with a price. The newest team proved a winner as Waltrip drove to his first career victory in the Daytona 500 but it was the race in which Earnhardt Sr. would lose his life.

Saddened but soldiering on "Little E", as he had come to be known, won when the tour returned to Daytona in July and again at Dover and Talladega to move into a top ten points finish for the season.

As Dale Earnhardt envisioned in 1982, his company has worked its way up through the ranks, winning races and championships by forming a strong foundation and building upon that. It is a philosophy that has made DEI a winner.

The Circuits

There have been a variety of facilities which have hosted **NASCAR**'s big time circuit, the Winston Cup Series. Some as short as one-fifth of a mile others as long as 4.2 miles. Some dirt, some paved, some flat, some high-banked. Each has a personality of its own.

Lowe's Motor Speedway at Charlotte

From near financial ruin to status as a showcase for stock car racing is the gamut run by the mile-and-a-half of asphalt known as Lowe's Motor Speedway at Charlotte. From the time co-founders Curtis Turner and Bruton Smith agreed to build it in 1959 until its emergence as one of the top tracks in NASCAR, the path has been a roller coaster journey.

From ground breaking in July 1959 until the first race the following June, work was frantic. Under-financed (as were many such endeavors of that era) and delayed by weather and geology, the construction progressed. Even the concept for the opening event was questioned. Rather than another 500-mile race like Darlington and Daytona offered, Turner and Smith decided to afford fans the longest race of the year to provide premiums not only on speed but durability as well. They thought of a 501-mile race with the checkered flag falling on the back stretch but discarded the concept in favor of a 600-miler. It would be something untried in the sport's annals.

Construction continued right into the opening time trials, as great quantities of rock were encountered where the farm field was thought to be only dirt. The untested paving did not stand up to the pounding of the cars. The race teams put deflectors on their hoods to protect the windshields from flying asphalt, and hung wire grates on the front of the cars to shield radiators, but the race ran.

Five dozen cars, aligned three abreast, took the starting flag. Less than a third of them were still racing at the end as unsung Joe Lee Johnson made up the deficit and took command for the final 48 laps. He was first under the checkered flag, five-and-a-half hours after the start.

A smaller than expected crowd led to the track's reorganization under Federal Bankruptcy laws. It survived and has grown to become a pioneer facility in racing. Now luxurious corporate suites overlook the track, as do condominiums. Seating of over 100,000 would swallow the 35,000 who saw the first event and the 600s now take less than four hours to complete. The May classic is now one of the four major events which count toward The Winston $Million and is still the longest distance event of each NASCAR season.

Durability has also improved through the intervening years. The 1996 running saw three-quarters of the starting field of 43 running at the end. Pole speeds are now in excess of 180mph on a track that saw the legendary Fireball Roberts earn the track's initial top qualifying honors at just over 130.

The track was designed with a unique double dog-leg front stretch which allows an unusual vantage point for spectators. Its quad oval design has seen as many as 54 lead changes since the 1979 edition of its 600. Although the 600 is the longest race, it has supplied first victories for some drivers. David Pearson (1960), Jeff Gordon (1994), and Bobby Labonte (1995) all recorded their initial career victories on the track which came full cycle from its troubled start to center stage among the event's tracks.

Great competition makes for sell-out crowds at all NASCAR tracks

4 CHARLOTTE 4

Darlington Raceway

NASCAR's first speedway and first paved track was South Carolina's Darlington Raceway

It was a bold experiment in 1950. Building a big paved track for stock car racing led some to think Harold Brasington a bit daft. But to do it in a tobacco field in rural South Carolina, as Brasington did, made most people think he'd really gone off the deep end.

Undaunted, he worked on the mile-and-a-quarter, egg-shaped oval, piling up dirt for banked turns when most of the western end had to have a narrower radius, since he hadn't been able to buy the land where the fishing pond lay outside of turn two. The sweeping third and fourth turn at the far end to the east resulted in being more than the normal 180-degrees as a result. And he planned to top the dirt with asphalt (all the tracks at the time had dirt surfaces!). But build it Brasington did.

He aimed for opening the traditional Labor Day weekend of 1950 and met his self-imposed deadline. But when he announced his plan for the race the doubters were more certain than ever that he was crazy.

'A 500-mile race? For stock cars'? Ol' Harold's been out in the sun too long,' was the most common reaction. With the assistance of big Bill France, they assembled a 75-car field to race for the $25,000 in prize money. Qualifying took two weeks. Curtis Turner was the pole winner at 82.034mph, but his mark was later topped by Wally Campbell at 82.40. Turner led the three-abreast field to the start but Gober Sosebee shot his Oldsmobile from the outside of the first row to be the event's initial lap leader.

Johnny Mantz, a veteran of AAA competition and the slowest qualifier for the event, employed hard rubber truck tires on the Plymouth he drove for Bill France and flagman Alvin Hawkins, and was the fourth and final race leader of the day. Mantz took the checkered flag with a nine-lap margin some six hours 38 minutes after the starting silk had waved. Fireball Roberts was second, with Red Byron third, despite running 24 tires off the rims of his Cadillac. Observers felt ol' Harold might be smarter than they had thought.

Some 82 cars representing a record 16 makes were on the grid for the second running on Labor Day in 1951, the largest and most diverse field in the division's history. Marshall Teague started 47th and rim-rode the track in his Hudson, taking the lead by the 13th lap in one of the most amazing charges in the sport's history. Although later sidelined by one of the event's many accidents, Teague watched with pleasure as Herb Thomas drove Teague's other Hudson to victory by leading the event's final 294 laps.

Until the 2.5-mile Daytona track opened in 1959, Darlington was the only site of a 500-mile event for NASCAR's major league. It was the circuit's major event, and the track's design makes it one of the most challenging even today, though the bankings have been elevated and the track now measures 1.366 miles in length. It is still the egg-shaped demon which challenged the sport's pioneers with their initial paved surface and inaugural 500-mile race—a track 'Too Tough To Tame.' It is the oldest big track event on the schedule and one of four which are included in The Winston $Million challenge, even though the 1997 Labor Day weekend's 500 saw the track flip-flopped with the front stretch now on what has been the back since 1950.

Harold Brasington had a good idea after all.

Daytona International Speedway

In the mid-1950s, Bill France had a dream of moving his races off the sands of Daytona Beach and onto a big, fast, high-banked track. It took him nearly five years to garner local approval and obtain financing, and construction was accomplished in a cypress swamp near the airport on the undeveloped western side of the city. But it was a magnificent temple of speed when completed and opened in 1959.

Huge 31-degree turns, a 'D' shaped front straight, and 3,000-foot-long back straightaway were unique features of the facility. It was wide and fast, designed for speed and close competition. It proved itself in the inaugural running of the Daytona 500 in 1959.

Cotton Owens was the top qualifier for that first race, with a speed of 143.198mph when the fastest lap at Darlington hadn't reached the 120mph level. Fifty-nine cars started the race which ran caution-free and resulted in a photo finish between Lee Petty's Oldsmobile and the Thunderbird piloted by Johnny Beauchamp. No one, even France, expected such a dramatic and close finish. Examining still photos and newsreel footage took three days before Petty was declared the event's winner.

Two winters later, Marvin Panch would drive a year-old Smokey Yunick Pontiac to victory in the prestigious event, doing so at an average speed of 149.601mph, identical to the third decimal point to the fastest lap turned in during Indy 500 qualifying the prior year. Even more recognition fell on France's track and his premier circuit. Not only did they afford close competition but they were fast, too.

Many feel the 1979 Daytona 500 was a turning point for the sport of stock car racing. It was run on a dank, overcast day when most of the eastern US was snow-covered. It was also the first event which CBS TV committed to cover flag-to-flag. Despite a weather-delayed start, the race was close and dramatic. The TV ratings swelled as the event progressed. Snowed-in fans called friends to tell them of this great race they were watching. The friends turned their sets to the race.

The race ended with the two leaders, Cale Yarborough and Donnie Allison, wrecking together for the

The crowd towers above the track
in the season opening Daytona 500

second time in the event as they headed for the checkered flag on the last lap. Richard Petty swept by the melee and onto his sixth of a record seven victories in the circuit's most important event.

The 1983 edition of the 500 saw an event record 59 lead changes, and the following year Cale Yarborough became the first to break the 200mph plateau on the track, only to flip his Oldsmobile while trying to enhance it further on his second qualifying lap. His mark was raised to 210.364mph by Bill Elliott in 1987 trials before speeds were reduced in a concession to safety.

Timing has helped the event's prestige. Since 1982, the 500 has served as the opening event of the Winston Cup season and runs at a time of year when most motorsports in the country are idled by winter's grip. From the track's 24-hour sports car event in late January through the year's biggest motorcycle races in mid-March, the speedway is the focus of racing in America, with the Daytona 500 the crowning jewel of France's dream.

Daytona's Beach-Road Course

When the world land speed record runs moved from the Florida sands in Daytona to the Salt Flats of Utah after Sir Malcolm Campbell's 1935 276.8mph run, the area was in danger of losing motorsports. The runs had been a mecca for tourism and brought international fame to the area. The city fathers sought something to replace the straight runs up and down the tide-packed sands.

A stock car race, sponsored by the city, appeared to be the answer. Bill France was merely a participant but liked the idea. The event, run north on a unique mile-and-a-half straightaway on the beach and returning south on the two-lane asphalt parallel length of highway A1A, was held with modest success in 1936. Although the promotion lost money, it drew people back to the area and maintained the reputation for racing. Events continued on the course until interrupted by World War II.

Peace brought a resumption of racing on the one-of-a-kind layout with the track refurbished and interest rekindled after five years

of hostilities. France, now both driving and promoting the events, watched them grow.

Growing too was home and motel construction in the surrounding area. Coinciding with the 1948 beginning of NASCAR, the track was moved several miles south on the ocean front peninsula and the track lengthened to a 4.2-mile circuit. Two miles up the beach to a tenth-mile limestone turn through the sand dunes it went, then two miles back south on the asphalt road to another tenth mile hairpin turn by the Ponce Inlet lighthouse back onto the sand. It was the design which first carried the cars in competition under the NASCAR banner and held the second event for the 'Strictly Stock' division which would evolve into the Winston Cup Series of today.

The circuit was also used for the annual AMA motorcycle racers.

All the NASCAR divisions, Modified, Sportsman, Convertible, and Winston Cup, fought the rutted turns, variable beach conditions and incoming tides over the ensuing 11 seasons. The final auto race on the track ran February 23, 1958, with Paul Goldsmith emerging victorious in a Smokey Yunick-prepared Pontiac. Goldsmith had won on the track in motorcycle racing previously but will be remembered as the last driver to win an auto race on the singular beach road course before the big paved track opened a few miles inland the following winter.

Totally unique was the sand and asphalt of the track on the beach in Daytona

Indianapolis Motor Speedway

The arrival of NASCAR's major league at the renowned 'Brickyard' in 1994 was a spectacular moment in the history of stock car racing. Here were the Fords, Chevrolets, and Pontiacs on the famed surface which had previously entertained the great opened wheel cars of AAA, USAC, and CART. Drivers named Earnhardt, Jarrett, Bodine and Wallace would race on the heretofore sacred surface where Foyt, Unser, Rose, and Vukovich had battled since the first Indy 500 in 1911.

NASCAR's biggest-ever crowd came at Indy's hallowed oval

There had been some testing of the waters before that inaugural 1994 'Brickyard 400' was slated. Two seasons earlier, a handful of NASCAR's top talent had come there from a 'tire test' after a race at Michigan. Thousands were waiting when they arrived and cheered as they took their first tentative laps around the famed two-and-a-half mile rectangular strip of historic asphalt.

The following season, an open test session was held and even more fans were on hand as the cars raced, diced, and drafted on the long straights, through the four 90-degree corners and in the short chutes where the high-pitched whine of Offenhausers was replaced by the guttural roar of the unmuffled V-8 engines. It was a show that proved to the few remaining doubters that NASCAR's machines could race on the flat quadrangle.

They came in 1994 to race. The richest event in the sport's history drew the largest crowd ever to witness them compete. They saw Rick Mast, who once traded a cow for his first race car, lead the 43-car field to their double file start by virtue of just the second pole of his career. The drivers thrilled themselves as they raced on the track most had grown up hearing of but doubted they'd ever race on. They thrilled the crowd, too, as 13 of the starters led the race and exchanged the lead 21 times during the 160 laps. Jeff Gordon went on to a half-second victory over Brett Bodine and a NASCAR record payday of $613,000 before an estimated 300,000 wildly cheering fans.

The race was a grand success for the track, the fans, the teams, and NASCAR. Once more they had ventured into an uncharted arena to successfully display the brand and quality of competition which has led the sport to unprecedented heights of success. But in doing so they didn't diminish the allure and magic of the Memorial Day 500, which for more than four score years had dominated American racing.

The NASCAR teams were back in 1995 and so were the fans. This time they saw Dale Earnhardt's black Chevy beat out Ford-mounted Rusty Wallace by a third of a second to take the richest race payoff of his career. The third time the NASCAR stars ran across the remaining yard of bricks at the track's finish line it was second generation driver Dale Jarrett leading his Yates Racing teammate Ernie Irnan after the 400 miles. Three races and as many different winners. Ricky Rudd made it four for four by winning the 1997 event, but the list ended there as Gordon became the first to repeat with a 1998 victory and Dale Jarrett won the sixth race at the track en route to the 1999 title.

Some traditionalists were horrified when the 'taxi cabs' of NASCAR announced they would race at Indy. Most have learned the race complements, not competes with, their open-wheeled machines of May, and American motorsports has been the biggest winner.

Michigan International Speedway

If there has been a track designed and built for great racing, to many fans and competitors feel it is this 'D'-shaped two-mile tri-oval with its 18-degree corner bankings. Wide and smooth, the facility is situated just an hour's drive west of America's automobile capital of Detroit.

The track was built in 1968 by Larry LoPatin's American Raceways, who employed Charles Moneypenny of Daytona Beach to design a perfect track. Moneypenny had been the designer of the Daytona and Talladega tracks (he would later design Richmond's new three-quarter-mile track, also.) Having left his engineering tables in Florida by oversight, Moneypenny utilized materials available at the Detroit library. Those were materials employed in the design of railroads with the required smooth transitions into and out of turns. 'Why not?' he thought, and proceeded with the project. The results proved themselves.

The track had run some sports car and Indy races in 1968 but the big NASCAR boys came in 1969. That season saw the most new tracks come onto the circuit. In addition to the Michigan facility, first time races were held that year at Dover, Delaware, Talladega, Alabama and at a new Texas facility in Bryan, similar to MIS and also owned by LoPatin's group.

The initial NASCAR event here was the Motor State 500, run in mid-June. Donnie Allison was the inaugural pole winner via a 160.135 mph lap, but outside front-row starter LeeRoy Yarborough took the lead in the initial lap to trigger the first of 35 changes of command during the 250 laps. That created a lead change every seven laps during the race that saw frequent three- and four-wide battles for position and which had a spectacular finish.

Cale Yarborough, driving the Wood brothers' Mercury, and Yarborough, in Junior Johnson's Ford, swapped four times in the final 30 laps. They were still side-by-side when they got the one-lap-to-go signal in the front stretch oval. Entering the first turn for the final time, the cars made contact. The white Ford went up the banking and slapped the wall, breaking the steering. Yarborough continued on in the Mercury and slid along the wall before grinding to a stop a hundred yards shy of the finish line. Listed as fourth in the final race rundown, Yarborough climbed from his crumpled machine to a standing ovation from a crowd who'd barely used their seats during the hotly contested event.

Two months later, the NASCAR stars were back for the inaugural 'Yankee 600', but that one held just 26 lead changes, plus much of the side-by-side battles in the 330 miles run before a steady Michigan rain brought the event to a premature close, with David Pearson driving a Holman-Moody Ford into a soggy victory celebration.

The following year and all the races since have run at a 200-lap, 400-mile distance, but even those have seen as many as 63 lead changes and still feature three-, four-, and five-wide battles for position in events that have seen the pole speeds top the 185 mph level.

Drafting, speed and competition have made the Michigan track among the most popular stops on the tour with both the competitors and fans. Its location in the Irish Hills vacation area of the state, so synonymous with the auto industry, has only added to the significance of the events held on the track that served as a primary pattern for current owner Roger Penske's new California track, which opened in '97.

Michigan: A stock car showcase in the midwest

Watkins Glen International

Few oval tracks and no other major road circuit in the country can claim the longevity in NASCAR's big time circuit as the twisting facility in the picturesque Finger Lakes area of upstate New York.

The Watkins Glen course was long noted as the site of the United States Grand Prix where the great cars and drivers of Formula One made their solitary American appearance. Now it is the site of the largest spectator event in the state of New York, a reputation earned by the crowds attracted to the Winston Cup race held here annually since 1986. But the NASCAR association dates back nearly three decades earlier.

In 1957, NASCAR cars first challenged the track. Buck Baker, a former bus driver from Charlotte, North Carolina, would lead a 20-car field into the event in his Chevrolet. The pole winner at 83.064 mph, Baker led the start and every lap as he nosed Fireball Roberts' Ford at the finish.

Historic note: The same day Baker was winning here, Parnelli Jones was winning his first NASCAR event on a road course at Bremerton, Washington. In that era of NASCAR racing, it was not uncommon for two of its major league events to run at the same time on each coast.

The big machines of NASCAR were back at the Glen's track twice in the 1960s, with Billy Wade winning the 1964 visit and Marvin Panch, who'd been Baker's chief challenger a decade earlier, winning in 1965.

Twenty-one years passed before the NASCAR teams came back to Watkins Glen. By then the Formula I event was no longer racing there and the track and that area of the state were economically depressed. Bill France, Jr, having succeeded his father as head of NASCAR and the International Speedway Corporation which owned the Daytona, Talladega and Darlington tracks, was approached to have his major circuit return to boost the track and region. ISC worked out a management agreement with the track, made improvements, and slated the return with brewing giant Anheuser-Busch's Budweiser brand as the major race sponsor.

The result was a huge success. For the opening day of practice a crowd was on hand larger than any event at the track had drawn since the departure of the Grand Prix. Race day was even larger and the hulking stock cars roared around the serpentine asphalt. They raced side by side, changing gears and braking as the fans crowded every vantage point. Tim Richmond drove Rick Hendrick's Chevrolet to victory in the return appearance.

The Glen's races have grown since. Rusty Wallace and Ricky Rudd have triumphed on the demanding track. So have Ernie Irvan and Kyle Petty—the latter's grandfather Lee raced in the '57 event. Mark Martin is a three-time Glen winner and the 1996 edition was won by Geoff Bodine, who grew up in nearby Chemung, New York, and had climbed a tree on the backstretch as a child to get a better view of the 1957 inaugural NASCAR event.

The track and area have rebounded from the depressed economics since this has become a regular stop on the Winston Cup schedule, with the annually-growing crowds drawn here by the competitive battles of NASCAR's stars running atop the faded Grand Prix tire tracks of drivers like Sterling Moss, Jackie Stewart, and Innes Ireland.

Pocono International Raceway

Each of today's Winston Cup tracks is different. Every one has its own characteristics. Perhaps none is more unlike any other than the three-turn triangular Pocono International Raceway in the lush Pocono resort area of Pennsylvania.

Once described as an oval built by committee, the 2.5-mile track has hosted NASCAR's premier division since 1974 and challenged the adaptability of both drivers and crews ever since. Each of its three straights is a different length and the three turns have a different radius and are banked at different angles. Despite the track's individuality, the competition found in the two annual 500 races is among the best of the year as seen in the total 49 lead changes during its two 1999 events.

Originally billed as the "Daytona of the North" due to both being the same length, the track ran one race a year for its first eight seasons and added the second race in 1982. Through the 1990s, the two races were held less than two months apart and presented in the closest proximity to each other among all of the tracks visited twice annually.

Ford-mounted Buddy Baker was the pole winner for NASCAR's inaugural event at the track in 1974. His top qualifying lap of 144.122 miles an hour took more than a minute to complete. A quarter century later found Chevrolet chauffeur Sterling Marlin holding the tracks time trial record at 170.506 mph. It took Marlin ten seconds less to complete his qualifying run in 1999 than it had Baker.

The track's wide front stretch extends 3,740 feet and is often the scene of five or six abreast racing. It leads to the 14-degree banking of the first turn, the steepest of the three. Exiting turn one, the cars enter the Long Pond Straight's 3,055 foot path to the eight degree banking of the second corner or "Tunnel Turn", so named because of the infield-access vehicle tunnel which runs under it. The shortest straight, at 1,780 feet, is the North Straight which connects the Tunnel turn to turn three which is, at six degrees, the flattest of the trio.

The uniqueness of Pocono's design, partially created by former Indy 500 winner, Roger Ward, makes it the only big track on the circuit where many drivers elect to shift gears during every lap. By doing so, they can opt for a gear ratio which allows them better acceleration out of the flat third turn, shift up at the start-finish line and shift down before entering the first turn. Before developing this tactic, many drivers over revved their engines as they wound them up down the lengthy straight.

The track's configuration is a cause for consternation for the mechanics responsible for the chassis set-up. The spring and shock absorber combination which get the car smoothly through the flat banking of the third turn, may not work in the steeper banking of the first corner. What helps a car through the intermediate second turn may not assist it in the other two. The successful drivers and crews, like four-time Pocono winners, Darrell Waltrip and Bill Elliott, or five-time pole winner, Ken Schrader, can create a "compromise" set up for the car and their driving style. Such a balance is not perfect for any turn, but allows them to get through each of the three efficiently. Such a balance was found in 1999 by Bobby Labonte and his Jimmy Maler-led team as they became the first to win both of the Pocono events during a season in more than a dozen years.

After a quarter century the track is still run by the Doctors Mattioli—Dr Joe, a retired Philadelphia dentist, and his wife, Dr Rose, who retired from a career as a podiatrist—who founded the facility. After nurturing it through its growing pains, the Doctors now share the daily operations with a dedicated staff which includes their children and grandchildren.

Despite the tracks one-of-a-kind design, Pocono has something in common with the other NASCAR Winston Cup tracks. It is beset with fans anxious for admission on every race day.

Pocono: a 2.5-mile challenge

Texas Motor Speedway

Despite its size, the 1997 opening of the mile-and-a-half Texas Motor Speedway was just the third site of NASCAR's major league competition in the Lone Star state. Previously, there had been Winston Cup races held at the half-mile Joseph Meyer Speedway in Houston and the two-mile Texas World Speedway at College Station, but there had been a 16-year absence of the sport since the roar of stock cars filled the Texas skies.

The new track, similar in design to the tracks at Charlotte and Atlanta's remodelled configuration with a double-dog-leg front stretch and 24-degree banking, was located near the Fort Worth suburb of Roanoke. It provided NASCAR, series and team sponsors with their first opportunity in nearly two decades to promote their names and products in the lucrative Dallas-Fort Worth region of the country.

It opened with a uniqueness not shared by any of the other tracks on the circuit. There was no initial pole winner for the inaugural Winston Cup race. Dale Jarrett started on the pole, but it was a position he was assigned as the early season point leader when rains curtailed practice and qualifying for the opening 500-mile event. NASCAR officials elected to use what track time was available for practice and familiarization runs on the facility and forego time trials. The 500's field was aligned in accordance with the Rule Book: the first 30 spots to the top 30 cars in the points standings, followed by former Series winners, former champions and the balance of the line-up set by the reception dates of entry forms at NASCAR headquarters in Florida.

That weekend's companion Busch Series race had been able to hold time trials the day before the torrents peppered the track. They, too, were unique in that series' history as the top speed of the session ended in a tie between two cars. Both Jeff Green and Elliott Sadler completed their 1.5-mile laps in 29.991 seconds for identical speeds of 180.054 miles an hour. It was the first time there had been a dead heat for the pole since NASCAR formed the Busch division in 1982. It had only happened once in Winston Cup competition when both Cale Yarborough and Charlie Glotzbach recorded the same time and speed for the pole during time trials for the 1968 Southern 500 at Darlington Raceway. In the 1960s, such ties were broken by preference to the car that recorded it first, thus

The 1997 opening ended a
16-year absence from Texas

Glotzbach was that event's pole winner. It was before your author created a drawing to determine the order of qualifying events (now used for all NASCAR touring series). The pole for the first Busch race ever held in Texas went to Green as driver of the car ranked higher in the owner points which is how such ties during time trials are now broken.

Although the track looked like Charlotte's layout, the teams quickly found out it was quite different. The radius of the Texas turns is longer than its North Carolina counterpart. The back stretch is shorter as are the short chutes that exit the fourth turn and lead to the first. Corner speeds are higher. Entry and exit points of the turns are different as is the line through the tricky front stretch.

The reduced practice and the tricky design showed up quickly when the inaugural race began on April 6, 1997. The first wreck occurred in the first turn of the first lap and involved 13 of the 43 cars which started the 500-mile chase and marked the Winston Cup return to Texas. Before Jeff Burton took the checkered flag to become the initial winner, there would be nine more yellow flags and 14 of the starters watched the end of the race as spectators.

The second year found the drivers more familiar with the track's layout with Mark Martin, Jeff Burton's team mate in the Jack Roush Ford stable, winning after fewer caution periods and lower attrition. The track's third season, 1999, found native Texan, Terry Labonte, affording Chevrolet an initial Texas triumph.

Huge crowds witnessed all three races to show the delight fans found in the long-awaited return of NASCAR to the Lone Star State.

New for NASCAR in June 1997

California Speedway

When the low-banked, two-mile California Speedway held its inaugural NASCAR Winston Cup race in June 1997, it returned stock car racing's most successful and competitive series to the heavily populated Los Angeles area and it moved the host state into a second-place tie among the 37 states which have been the sites of NASCAR's major league. The track, a D-shaped tri-oval which resembles Michigan Speedway, is the 15th venue in the Golden State where the sport has raced and is the third super speedway.

The successful reclamation of the track site at Fontana, California, from a contaminated former steel mill to a sports facility made the state rank only behind North Carolina in the number of facilities where the big-time cars of NASCAR have run. North Carolina can list 28 such tracks in the sport's history. California now rates second on the list tied with New York which also found the major league at 15 different arenas over the years.

The other big ovals in California's motorsports history are the 1.4-mile Marchbanks Speedway in Hanford where they raced briefly in the early 1960s and the now-defunct Ontario Motor Speedway, a 2.5-mile quad-oval similar to Indianapolis, where they competed nine times during the 1970s.

The Ontario site was just a few miles west of the new track's locale. The new track is just 20 miles away from the now-closed road circuit of Riverside International Raceway where they raced into the 1988 season.

The first NASCAR pole winner here was Joe Nemechek, but he established a qualifying record which lasted just one day. The pole was won at 183.015 when time trials began NASCAR competition on the track. The following day, in the second qualifying session, his mark was bettered by Greg Sacks at 183.753. It is rare for the pole winner not to be the fastest, but not unheard of. It is as old as NASCAR's speedway racing and first found at Darlington's original race in 1950. Then it was Curtis Turner winning the pole only to have his speed later bettered by Wally Campbell. Daytona's first 500 saw Bob Welborn as the pole winner, but the fast time trial honor went to Cotton Owens. Another lies at Talladega when first pole winner Bobby Isaac saw his speed exceeded later by Charlie Glotzbach for the inaugural Alabama event. This was the last such instance before California Speedway's.

Race fans may see a similarity in California Speedway to the two-mile oval at Michigan, but looks can be deceiving. The Michigan track, which was also owned by Roger Penske, has 18-degree banking in the sweeping turns and is sloped up 12 in the tri-oval area of the front stretch. Its California sister has corner banking of 14 degrees and the start-finish line is one degree less than the midwestern counterpart. The backstraight here is 3,100 feet long, 900 more than Michigan's. The front stretch here is 1,100 feet less. Despite the deviations, speeds at the two tracks are similar, with both sites qualifying records in the mid-180 miles per hour range and both facilities lend themselves to three or four wide battles for position.

In 1999, all of the Penske tracks, including both this one and the Michigan facility, were taken into the International Speedway Corporation to add to their ownership of Daytona, Talladega, Darlington and other tracks.

Jeff Gordon, a native of Vallejo, California, was the track's first winner as he took a one-second victory margin over his Hendricks Motorsports team mate, Terry Labonte, in the 1997 inaugural running of the California 500. Mark Martin won the race in its second running the next season, and in 1999 Gordon became the first driver to win the race for a second time. Gordon's second victory continued the string of shut-outs for the event's pole winners. Victory for Gordon and Martin both came after starting third in the field. Gordon's second triumph was launched from fifth place in the starting line-up.

The opening of California Speedway and the presentation of these Winston Cup events are the continuation of the sport at California ovals which dates back to April 1951, when Daytona's Marshall Teague drove a Hudson Hornet to victory on the half-mile dirt track at Gardena. Teague's win began nearly half a century of NASCAR competition in the country's most-populated state.

The biggest and fastest on the scene

... Earnhardt had won nine of the ... races at the facility entered its fourth ... A second 500-mile annual race was ... the races schedule in 1970.) Included in ... a sweep of the two races held there ... to equal his 1990 performance. ... those many seasons have been able ... the track in a season. The first do to ... Hamilton in 1970, followed by Buddy Baker ... Waltrip in 1982, before Earnhardt's

... troubled beginning, the track has ... the most exciting on the circuit. As the ... half century it finds that four of the ... competitive races have been presented here, ... the 1984 race which saw 75 lead changes ... was required to cover 500 miles. The track, ... located on the site of a World War II airfield, also ... of most drivers to lead any race in ... That track was set in the second 1986 race ... drivers had at some point during the event. ... hallmarks of the track since its ... first qualified on the track at ... to set the all-time NASCAR mark. ... trouble with the imposition of ... plates for safety after Bobby Allison's ... over the retaining fence in the race ... Despite the deterrent to speed, ... saw Mark Martin average ... 500 miles to win the fastest ... NASCAR's history.

... cars racing three and four abreast, ... Talladega as the white knuckled ... for positions before more than

Statistics

Year	Car No.	Champion Driver	Champion Owner	Make Car	Race Wins
1949a	22	Red Byron	Raymond Parks	Oldsmobile	2
1950b	60	Bill Rexford	Julian Buesink	Oldsmobile	1
1951	92	Herb Thomas	Herb Thomas	Hudson	7
1952	91	Tim Flock	Ted Chester	Hudson	8
1953	92	Herb Thomas	Herb Thomas	Hudson	11
1954	92	-	Herb Thomas*	Hudson	12
	42	Lee Petty	-	Chrysler	7
1955	300	Tim Flock	Carl Kiekhaefer	Chrysler	18
1956	300B	Buck Baker	Carl Kiekhaefer	Chrysler	14
1957	87	Buck Baker	Buck Baker	Chevrolet	10
1958	42	Lee Petty	Petty Entrp.	Oldsmobile	7
1959	42	Lee Petty	Petty Entrp.	Plymouth	10
1960	4	Rex White	White-Clements	Chevrolet	6
1961	11	Ned Jarrett	W.G. Holloway, Jr	Chevrolet	1
1962	8	Joe Weatherly	Bud Moore	Pontiac	9
1963	21	-	Wood Brothers*	Ford	3
	8	Joe Weatherly*	-	Mercury	3
1964	43	Richard Petty	Petty Entrp.	Plymouth	9
1965	11	Ned Jarrett	Bondy Long	Ford	13
1966	6	David Pearson	Cotton Owens	Dodge	14
1967	43	Richard Petty	Petty Entrp.	Plymouth	27
1968	17	David Pearson	Holman-Moody	Ford	16
1969	17	David Pearson	Holman-Moody	Ford	11
1970	71	Bobby Isaac	Nord Krauskopf	Dodge	11
1971	43	Richard Petty	Petty Entrp.	Plymouth	21
1972c	43	Richard Petty	Petty Entrp.	Plymouth	8
1973	72	Benny Parsons	L.G. DeWitt	Chevrolet	1
1974	43	Richard Petty	Petty Entrp.	Dodge	10

1975	43	Richard Petty	Petty Entrp.	Dodge	13
1976	11	Cale Yarborough	Junior Johnson	Chevrolet	9
1977	11	Cale Yarborough	Junior Johnson	Chevrolet	9
1978	11	Cale Yarborough	Junior Johnson	Oldsmobile	10
1979	43	Richard Petty	Petty Entrp.	Chevrolet	5
1980	2	Dale Earnhardt	Rod Osterlund	Chevrolet	5
1981	11	Darrell Waltrip	Junior Johnson	Buick	12
1982	11	Darrell Waltrip	Junior Johnson	Buick	12
1983	22	Bobby Allison	Bill Gardner	Buick	6
1984	44	Terry Labonte	Billy Hagan	Chevrolet	2
1985	11	Darrell Waltrip	Junior Johnson	Chevrolet	3
1986	3	Dale Earnhardt	Richard Childress	Chevrolet	5
1987	3	Dale Earnhardt	Richard Childress	Chevrolet	11
1988	9	Bill Elliott	Harry Melling	Ford	6
1989	27	Rusty Wallace	Raymond Beadle	Pontiac	6
1990	3	Dale Earnhardt	Richard Childress	Chevrolet	9
1991	3	Dale Earnhardt	Richard Childress	Chevrolet	4
1992	7	Alan Kulwicki	Alan Kulwicki	Ford	2
1993	3	Dale Earnhardt	Richard Childress	Chevrolet	6
1994	3	Dale Earnhardt	Richard Childress	Chevrolet	4
1995	24	Jeff Gordon	Rick Hendrick	Chevrolet	7
1996	5	Terry Labonte	Rick Hendrick	Chevrolet	2
1997	24	Jeff Gordon	Rick Hendrick	Chevrolet	10
1998	24	Jeff Gordon	Rick Hendrick	Chevrolet	13
1999	88	Dale Jarrett	Robert Yates	Ford	4
2000	18	Bobby Labonte	Joe Gibbs Racing	Pontiac	4
2001	24	Jeff Gordon	Rick Hendrick	Chevrolet	6

Won Driver or Owner Championship; a= known as Strictly Stock Division; b= renamed Grand National Division; c= renamed Winston Cup Series.

ALL-TIME WINSTON CUP RACE WINNERS *(1949–2001)*

Rank	Driver	Wins
1	Richard Petty*	200
2	David Pearson*	105
3	Darrell Waltrip	84
	Bobby Allison*	84
5	Cale Yarborough*	83
6	Dale Earnhardt#	76
7	Jeff Gordon	58
8	Lee Petty*	54
	Rusty Wallace	54
10	Junior Johnson*	50
	Ned Jarrett*	50
12	Herb Thomas#	48
13	Buck Baker*	46
14	Bill Elliott	41
15	Tim Flock#	40
16	Bobby Isaac#	37
17	Fireball Roberts#	34
18	Mark Martin	29
19	Dale Jarrett	28
20	Rex White*	26
	Fred Lorenzen*	26
22	Jim Paschal*	25
23	Joe Weatherly#	24
24	Ricky Rudd	22
25	Benny Parsons*	21
	Jack Smith*	21
	Terry Labonte	21
28	Speedy Thompson#	20
29	Buddy Baker*	19
	Fonty Flock#	19
	Davey Allison#	19
32	Harry Gant*	18
	Neil Bonnett#	18
	Geoff Bodine	18
35	Marvin Panch*	17
	Curtis Turner#	17
	Jeff Burton	17
38	Ernie Irvan*	15
39	Dick Hutcherson*	14
	LeeRoy Yarbrough#	14

*Retired #Deceased In the 1,950 races during the period there have been 162 drivers who have won at least one event.

ALL-TIME WINSTON CUP POLE WINNERS *(1949–2001)*

Rank	Driver	Poles
1	Richard Petty*	126
2	David Pearson*	113
3	Cale Yarborough*	70
4	Darrell Waltrip	59
5	Bobby Allison*	57
6	Bobby Isaac#	51
	Bill Elliott	51
8	Junior Johnson*	47
9	Buck Baker*	44
10	Mark Martin	41
11	Buddy Baker*	40
	Jeff Gordon	40
13	Herb Thomas*	39
	Tim Flock#	39
15	Geoff Bodine	37
16	Fireball Roberts#	35
	Ned Jarrett*	35
	Rex White*	35
19	Fonty Flock#	34
20	Fred Lorenzen*	33
21	Ricky Rudd	27
22	Terry Labonte	26
23	Jack Smith*	24
	Alan Kulwicki#	24
25	Ken Schrader	23
26	Dale Earnhardt	22
	Dick Hutcherson*	22

*Retired #Deceased

In the 1,944 races where time trials were held (or records kept), there have been 189 drivers who have won pole positions.

MOST COMPETITIVE RACES

Lead Rank	Race Event	Race Track	Changes	Winner	Laps
1	1984 Winston 500	Talladega, AL	75	Cale Yarborough	188
2	1984 Talladega 500	Talladega, AL	68	Dale Earnhardt	188
3	1978 Talladega 500	Talladega, AL	67	Lennie Pond	188
4	1981 Champion 400	Brooklyn, MI	65	Richard Petty	200
5	1977 Winston 500	Talladega, AL	63	Darrell Waltrip	188
6	1983 Daytona 500	Daytona, FL	59	Cale Yarborough	200
7	1979 Coca Cola 500	Pocono, PA	58	Cale Yarborough	200
8	1979 World 600	Charlotte, NC	54	Darrell Waltrip	400
9	1982 Winston 500	Talladega, AL	51	Darrell Waltrip	188
10	1986 Talladega 500	Talladega, AL	49	Bobby Hillin	188
	1989 DieHard 500	Talladega, AL	49	Terry Labonte	1881989
	2001 Daytona 500	Daytona, FL	49	Michael Waltrip	200

NOTE: *In the 1986 Talladega 500 a NASCAR record 26 different drivers, of the 42 who started, officially led during the event's 188 laps.*

2001 WINSTON CUP SEASON STANDINGS

Pos	Driver	Pts	Wins	Top-5	Top-10	Winnings
1	Jeff Gordon	5,112	6	18	24	$6,649,076
2	Tony Stewart	4,763	3	15	22	$3,493,043
3	Sterling Marlin	4,741	2	12	20	$3,361,662
4	Ricky Rudd	4,706	2	14	22	$3,976,203
5	Dale Jarrett	4,612	4	12	19	$4,608,366
6	Bobby Labonte	4,561	2	9	20	$4,139,851
7	Rusty Wallace	4,481	1	8	14	$4,272,406
8	Dale Earnhardt, Jr.	4,460	3	9	15	$5,384,627
9	Kevin Harvick	4,406	2	6	16	$3,716,633
10	Jeff Burton	4,394	2	8	16	$3,866,333
11	Johnny Benson	4,152	0	6	14	$2,573,569
12	Mark Martin	4,095	0	3	15	$3,487,719
13	Matt Kenseth	3,982	0	4	9	$2,265,739
14	Ward Burton	3,846	1	6	10	$3,293,599
15	Bill Elliott	3,824	1	5	9	$3,337,671
16	Jimmy Spencer	3,782	0	3	8	$2,398,939
17	Jerry Nadeau	3,675	0	4	10	$2,246,774
18	Bobby Hamilton	3,575	1	3	7	$2,275,904
19	Ken Schrader	3,480	0	0	5	$2,254,390
20	Elliott Sadler	3,471	1	2	2	$2,525,007
21	Ricky Craven	3,379	1	4	7	$1,923,981
22	Dave Blaney	3,303	0	0	6	$1,788,146
23	Terry Labonte	3,280	0	1	3	$2,972,901
24	Michael Waltrip	3,159	1	3	3	$3,373,394
25	Robert Pressley	3,156	0	1	5	$2,100,020

TOP-FIVE TEAM OWNERS FOR THE 2001 WINSTON CUP

1. **Roush Racing** (Ford) 15,552pts
No.99, Jeff Burton; No.6, Mark Martin; No.17, Matt Kenseth; No.97, Kurt Busch

2. **Hendrick Motorsports** (Chevrolet) 12,067pts
No.24, Jeff Gordon; No.5, Terry Labonte; No.25, Jerry Nadeau;

3. **Dale Earnhardt Incorporated** (Chevrolet) 10,478pts
No.1, Steve Park; No.8, Dale Earnhardt, Jr.; No.15, Michael Waltrip

4. **Joe Gibbs Racing** (Pontiac) 9,324pts
No.18, Bobby Labonte; No.20, Tony Stewart.

5. **Robert Yates Racing** (Ford) 6,435
No. 28, Ricky Rudd; No.88, Dale Jarrett

WINS BY CAR MAKE
(1949–2001)

Ford	517	Buick	65
Chevrolet	497	Chrysler	59
Plymouth	190	Thunderbird*	6
Dodge	168	AMC Matador	5
Pontiac	148	Lincoln	4
Oldsmobile	116	Studebaker	3
Mercury	96	Nash	1
Hudson	79	Jaguar	1

Thunderbird listed as separate make in 1959. Now included under Ford. Three other races won by Grand American Division cars (i.e. Chevrolet Camaro, Ford Mustang) in combined events not shown in above totals for 1,950 races.

TOP 20 MONEY WINNERS IN WINSTON CUP RACING (1949–Dec. 2001)

Rank	Driver	Career Starts	Career Winnings	Career Wins
1	Jeff Gordon	293	$45,566,580	58
2	Dale Earnhardt	676	$41,742,384	76
3	Dale Jarrett	459	$33,274,832	28
4	Rusty Wallace	526	$24,869,067	54
5	Mark Martin	494	$29,165,322	32
6	Bill Elliott	659	$27,506,174	41
7	Terry Labonte	709	$26,536,692	21
8	Bobby Labonte	294	$25,953,024	17
9	Ricky Rudd	731	$24,530,223	22
10	Jeff Burton	259	$22,958,499	17
11	Sterling Marlin	539	$19,899,539	8
12	Darrell Waltrip	809	$19,416,618	84
13	Ken Schrader	528	$18,124,281	4
14	Geoffrey Bodine	552	$14,831,269	18
15	Michael Waltrip	498	$14,829,876	1
16	Kyle Petty	609	$13,331,568	8
17	Ward Burton	250	$13,023,311	3
18	Bobby Hamilton	337	$12,990,059	4
19	Brett Bodine	442	$11,425,453	1
20	Ernie Irvan	292	$10,552,042	15

RACE RECORDS AT CURRENT WINSTON CUP TRACKS *(through the 2001 season)*

ATLANTA MOTOR SPEEDWAY (1.54 Mile/1960)
500 Miles: 159.904 mph by Bobby Labonte, Pontiac, Nov. 16, 1997

BRISTOL MOTOR SPEEDWAY (.533 Mile/1961)
500 Laps: 101.074 mph by Charlie Glotzbach, Chev., July 11, 1971

CALIFORNIA SPEEDWAY (2.0 Mile/1997)
500 miles: 155.012 mph by Jeff Gordon, Chev., June 22, 1997

CHICAGOLAND (1.5 Mile/2001)
400 miles: 121.200 mph by Kevin Harvick, Chev., July 15, 2001

DARLINGTON RACEWAY (1.366 Mile/1950)
500 Miles: 137.958 mph by Dale Earnhardt, Chev., March 28, 1993
400 Miles: 132.703 mph by David Pearson, Ford, May 11, 1968

DAYTONA INTERNATIONAL SPEEDWAY (2.5 Miles/1959)
500 Miles: 177.602 mph by Buddy Baker, Oldsmobile, Feb. 17, 1980
400 Miles: 173.473 mph by Bobby Allison, Mercury, July 4, 1980

DOVER DOWNS SPEEDWAY (1.0 Mile/1969)
400 Miles: 132.719 mph by Mark Martin, Ford, Sept. 21, 1997

INDIANAPOLIS MOTOR SPEEDWAY (2.5 Mile/1994)
400 Miles: 155.912 mph by Bobby Labonte, Pontiac, Aug. 5, 2000

KANSAS SPEEDWAY (1.5 Mile/2001)
400 Miles: 110.576 mph by Jeff Gordon, Chev. Sept. 30, 2001

LAS VEGAS MOTOR SPEEDWAY (1.5 Mile/1998)
400 Miles: 146.554 mph by Mark Martin, Ford, March 1, 1998

LOWE'S MOTOR SPEEDWAY AT CHARLOTTE (1.5 Mile/1960)
600 Miles: 151.952 mph by Bobby Labonte, Chev., May 28, 1995
500 Miles: 160.630 mph by Jeff Gordon, Chev., Oct. 11, 1999

MICHIGAN SPEEDWAY (2.0 Mile/1969)
400 Miles: 173.997 mph by Dale Jarrett, Ford, June 13, 1999

NEW HAMPSHIRE SPEEDWAY (1.058 Mile/1993)
300 Laps: 117.144 mph by Jeff Burton, Ford, July 13, 1997

NORTH CAROLINA SPEEDWAY (1.017 Mile/1965)
400 Miles: 131.103 mph by Jeff Burton, Ford, Oct. 24, 1999

PHOENIX INTERNATIONAL RACEWAY (1.0 Mile/1998)
312 Miles: 118.132 mph by Tony Stewart, Pontiac, Nov. 7, 1999

POCONO INTERNATIONAL RACEWAY (2.5 Mile/1974)
500 Miles: 144.892 mph by Rusty Wallace, Ford, July 21, 1996

RICHMOND INTERNATIONAL RACEWAY (.75 Mile/1953)
300 Miles: 108.707 mph by Dale Jarrett, Sept. 6, 1997

SEARS POINT RACEWAY (1.95 Mile Road Course/1989)
224 Miles: 75.889 mph by Tony Stewart, Pontiac, June 24, 2001

TALLADEGA SUPER SPEEDWAY (2.66 Mile/1969)
500 Miles: 188.354* mph by Mark Martin, Ford, May 10, 1997
* Fastest point race in NASCAR history.

TEXAS MOTOR SPEEDWAY (1.5 Mile/1997)
500 Miles: 144.276 mph by Terry Labonte, Chevy, March 28, 1999

WATKINS GLEN (2.45 Mile Road Course/1957)
220.5 Miles: 103.030 mph by Mark Martin, Ford, Aug. 9, 1996

Note: Information given in parenthesis: Track size/Year of first Winston Cup race.

POINT SYSTEM DISTRIBUTION
(For Winston Cup, Busch Grand National and Craftsman Truck Divisions)

1st..........175*	16th..........115	31st..........70	
2nd..........170	17th..........112	32nd..........67	
3rd..........165	18th..........109	33rd..........64	
4th..........160	19th..........106	34th..........61	
5th..........155	20th..........103	35th..........58	
6th..........150	21st..........100	36th..........55	
7th..........146	22nd..........97	37th..........52	
8th..........142	23rd..........94	38th..........49	
9th..........138	24th..........91	39th..........46	
10th..........134	25th..........88	40th..........43	
11th..........130	26th..........85	41st..........40	
12th..........127	27th..........82	42nd..........37	
13th..........124	28th..........79	43rd..........34	
14th..........120	29th..........76	44th..........31	
15th..........117	30th..........73	etc. by -3 per pos.	

BONUSES

Each race leader receives a five point bonus. The driver leading the most laps receives an additional five-point bonus with duplicate points awarded in case of a tie for most laps led. Both owners and starting drivers earn points.

*First place finisher must lead at least the last lap thus making first place worth a minimum of 180 points.

NOTE

Other NASCAR touring divisions utilize a similar system.

Chronology

1947 Organizational meeting convened by Bill France at Streamline hotel in Daytona Beach, Florida on December 14. NASCAR is formed.

1948 Initial NASCAR sanctioned race held February 15 on the beach-road course in Daytona Beach. Red Byron is the first winner. The incorporation is formalized February 21. The season consists of 52 Modified races with Red Byron emerging as the first champion.

1949 On June 19 NASCAR holds its first "Strictly Stock" race at Charlotte, N.C., with Jim Roper of Kansas winning in a Lincoln. The division would become the Winston Cup Series. Red Byron wins two of the season's eight races and becomes its inaugural champion.

1950 South Carolina's Darlington Raceway opens and hosts the first 500-mile race and the first paved track for the new car circuits now renamed "Grand National". Johnny Mantz wins it over a 75-car field in a Plymouth. NASCAR also begins group insurance coverage for competitors and officials. Tracks in the northeast come into the NASCAR fold and a Sportsman division is formed to lower the costs of competition at short tracks.

1952 NASCAR required roll bars in the cars.

1954 NASCAR expands to the Pacific coast and ten western tracks begin holding events under the sanctioning body's banner. Some 136 cars start the combined Modified-Sportsman race at Daytona. Bill France announces plans to move the races from the beach to a permanent track in Daytona.

1955 Herb Thomas wins the Southern 500 at Darlington for a third time to become the first driver to do so. The concepts of multi-car teams and sponsorships is introduced by Mercury Outboard's Carl Kiekhaefer and his fleet of Chryslers. The Grand National circuit expands to 45 events as presented at 32 tracks across the country.

1958 The final stock car race is run on Daytona's beach/road course with Paul Goldsmith winning in a Pontiac. construction is progressing on the new 2.5-mile high banked track west of the city. Lee Petty wins his second championship in a 51 race slate.

1959 Daytona Speedway opens with Lee Petty winning by inches over Johnny Beauchamp in a photo finish. Petty goes on to win an unprecedented third driving championship.

1960 NASCAR adds big, banked tracks at Atlanta and Charlotte to its race venues. Rex White wins the Grand National title.

1961 The July 4 Firecracker 250 race at Daytona Speedway becomes the first stock race shown on ABC-TV's "Wide World of Sports". David Pearson wins the race and two other big track events to be the first driver to win three in the sport's history. Ned Jarrett goes on to claim the season's crown.

1963 Fred Lorenzen wins six major races and becomes the first NASCAR driver to win more than $100,000 in a season.

1964 Goodyear tests and introduces the LifeGuard inner-liner for racing tires on the Grand National circuit.

1965 The fuel cell bladder is introduced by Firestone Tire and Rubber Company to diminish the threat of fire. North Carolina Motor Speedway opens at Rockingham with Curtis Turner the first winner on the one-mile oval.

1966 Four new big tracks, including the 2.66-mile, 33-degree banked Talladega Super Speedway, join the NASCAR family as racing shifts from short to big tracks. David Pearson becomes the second three time champion and the first to top $200,000 in one season winnings.

1970 Buddy Baker becomes the first stock car driver to exceed 200 miles an hour. He runs 200.447 in a special timed run at Talladega. The final dirt track race is held on a half-mile oval at Raleigh, North Carolina, with Richard Petty winning.

1971 The Grand National division becomes Winston Cup through sponsorship by R. J. Reynolds' Winston brand. Richard Petty wins his third championship and becomes the sport's first million dollar winner.

1972 Bill France, Sr., steps down as president of NASCAR as he hands the position to his son Bill Junior. The Winston Cup series is reduced to approximately 30 races a season, all major events.

1975 A new point system is used to determine the Winston Cup championship. Richard Petty uses it to win his sixth title.

1976 Buddy Baker becomes the first driver to win a 500-mile race in less than three hours as he takes the Winston 500 at Talladega in 2 hours, 56 minutes, 37 seconds (169.887 mph). The year also sees Winston Cup racing become the world-wide leader in racing attendance with 1.4 million spectators.

1978 NASCAR competitors and officials are hosted at the White House in Washington by President and Mrs. Jimmy Carter. Cale Yarborough becomes the first driver to win the Winston Cup crown three times consecutively.

1979 CBS-TV shows the Daytona 500 live from start to finish with Richard Petty winning and going on to his seventh title.

1980 Dale Earnhardt, the 1979 Rookie of the Year, wins his first Winston Cup championship marking the first time any driver has won the two distinctions back to back.

1981 Darrell Waltrip wins his second straight Winston Cup crown. The season saw 773 lead changes among 40 different drivers. Attendance is 1.55 million.

1982 NASCAR forms the Busch Series from the Late Model Stock division with sponsorship from Anheuser-Busch brand.

1984 Richard Petty wins an unprecedented 200th race as he takes the July Fourth race at Daytona with President Ronald Reagan in attendance.

1985 R. J. Reynolds announces "The Winston Million" bonus for a driver who wins three of the four biggest events of the season. The prize is claimed by Bill Elliott when he wins at Darlington. Darrell Waltrip wins his third title.

1992 Alan Kulwicki becomes the first owner-driver to earn the Winston Cup title since Buck Baker in 1957, as he wins it by ten points over Bill Elliott in the closest decision ever. Richard Petty drives his last career race in the season finale at Atlanta and newcomer Jeff Gordon makes his first start. NASCAR founder Bill France and his wife Anne both pass away.

1994 The inaugural Brickyard 400 NASCAR race is run at Indianapolis Motor Speedway with Jeff Gordon winning. Dale Earnhardt wins his seventh Winston Cup crown to tie Richard Petty on top of the all-time list.

1996 NASCAR expands overseas with an exhibition race in Japan. NASCAR goes downtown with the opening of NASCAR Thunder retails stores and NASCAR cafes. All Winston Cup races are televised live by network or cable systems.

1997 New super speedways at Texas and California join the circuit. Jeff Gordon becomes the second driver to win the Winston Cup Million with a victory at Darlington as he becomes the first to ever win the Southern 500 three consecutive times. Gordon goes on to win his second Winston Cup championship in a $6.3 million year.

1998 New Las Vegas track is added to schedule with Mark Martin the inaugural winner. Jeff Gordon wins 13 races, tieing a modern era record. Included is an unprecedented fourth straight Southern 500 at Darlington en route to a third Winston Cup championship in the last four years giving an also unprecedented fourth consecutive title for owner Rick Hendrick. Gordon wins a record $9.3 million.

1999 The 34-race schedule finds Jeff Gordon atop the winners list with seven victories and an equal number of poles but it is Dale Jarrett taking the Champion's trophy at season's end. Jarrett, a four-time race winner during the season, amasses $6.6 million in season earnings and becomes only the second son to follow his father as the champion of NASCAR biggest circuit. Ned Jarrett, Dale's father, won the title in 1961 and 1965. There were 11 different drivers feted in victory lanes during the campaign and 15 winning poles. The circuit added Homestead-Miami Speedway to its roster of tracks with Tony Stewart emerging at the first winner enroute to Rookie of the Year honors. Dale Earnhardt, Junior wins his second straight Busch Grand National crown.

2000 A season of consistency, including 19 top-5 finishes, hands the Winston Cup title to Bobby Labonte. Bobby and Terry Labonte become the first brothers to win Winston Cup titles. Fourth generation driver, Adam Petty, is fatally injured in a crash during Busch Series practice at New Hampshire International Speedway on May 12. Dale Earnhardt Jr bursts onto the Winston Cup scene with three victories.

2001 The new century and NASCAR's 54th season finds an ambitious 36-race schedule and a new television package for FOX and NBC-Turner for all Winston Cup races. The point fund is upped to $13 million and the champion's share jumps to $3.6-million. TV monies expand race purses above the $3 million mark, each. Over 40 drivers exceed the once unreachable Million dollar a year plateau in race winnings as Jeff Gordon, in just his ninth full season, tops the list by winning his fourth championship. He becomes only the third driver to win more than three as he joins only the retired Richard Petty and the late Dale Earnhardt. Motorsports loses one of its great drivers as Earnhardt dies in a final lap wreck in the season opening Daytona 500 as his cars, driven by Michael Waltrip and Earnhardt's son, Dale Junior, go on to a one-two finish, respectively, in the race. The season finds TV ratings soaring as 17 different drivers win and 18 take pole honors during the season. First time winners include Michael Waltrip, Kevin Harvick, Elliot Sadler and Ricky Craven. The circuit adds new tracks in Chicago and Kansas City to bring the total facilities hosting it to 168 in 36 states over the division's 53-year history. Harvick was the inaugural winner at Chicago with Jeff Gordon the first to win in Kansas.